P9-CQC-189

PLAYERS FIRST

PLAYERS FIRST

Coaching from the Inside Out

JOHN CALIPARI

AND MICHAEL SOKOLOVE

THE PENGUIN PRESS | *New York* | 2014

THE PENGUIN PRESS
Published by the Penguin Group
Penguin Group (USA) LLC
375 Hudson Street
New York, New York 10014

USA · Canada · UK · Ireland · Australia
New Zealand · India · South Africa · China

penguin.com
A Penguin Random House Company

First published by The Penguin Press, a member of Penguin Group (USA) LLC, 2014

Photograph credits appear on page 277.

ISBN 978-1-59420-573-6

Printed in the United States of America
1 3 5 7 9 10 8 6 4 2

Designed by Nicole LaRoche

In honor of two special women in my life—
my wife, Ellen, and my late mother, Donna.

CONTENTS

PLAYERS FIRST

THE NAMES ON THE BACKS OF THE JERSEYS

In my office at the University of Kentucky, I can stand in front of a huge window and look right down on the hardwood floor of our practice court. I can also see the eight banners representing eight national championships—from 1948, the first of Adolph Rupp's four titles, to 2012, the one we added to the collection.

One day I was looking through that window with John Robic, a Pittsburgh kid like me and one of my assistant coaches going all the way back to the University of Massachusetts, which ranked 295th among 300 NCAA Division I teams when we took over. We turned to each other and both said a version of the same thing: *Can you believe we're coaching at this place?*

Kentucky is arguably college basketball's most legendary program. It has the most wins and the most devoted fan base. (I call them crazy; they watch more game film than I do.) I respect the tradition—I'm lucky to be a part of it and I've got the best job in basketball. But my first priority isn't the Commonwealth of Kentucky, or the university, or the legacy of the program, or the greater glory of Big Blue Nation. There was a time I coached partly for myself—for status, respect, money, wins. I'm not immune to any of these things, but they're not really the point anymore, either. Good for those coaches who get to seven hundred, eight hundred, or even a thousand wins, but I'm not staying in it that long. I can promise you my record will not be on my tombstone.

I coach for the names on the backs of the jerseys—not just the front. My players. They are sent to me by their fathers, their mothers, their grandmothers, their aunts—whoever in this world raised them and loves them. Others look at their NBA bodies and consider them lucky. Future millionaires, just stopping through before they cash in. That's not what I see. They're kids, some of them as young as seventeen years old. They all need me in a different way. Some want my affection, others my approval. It's a burden to be responsible for other people's children, sometimes a heavy burden.

I go to Mass every morning. It's how I start my day and it's my moment of peace, almost meditation. If I'm struggling with a player, it's where I ask myself: *How would I want my own son treated?*

But I'm also a sinner, as we all are. If you come after one of my players, I come after you twice as hard. If you kill one of mine, I burn your village. It's the Italian in me. I'm not proud of that, but it's who I am.

became the Kentucky coach on April 1, 2009, after nine successful years at Memphis. When I was introduced at an on-campus press conference, our athletic director, Mitch Barnhart, said, "We quickly zeroed in on a coach, and frankly, he zeroed in on us, as well."

That was absolutely true. I'd dreamed of coaching at Kentucky ever since I took one of my Massachusetts teams to play at Rupp Arena. My friends, toward the end of my time at Memphis, were telling me that I deserved to be at a school that had a state as part of its name (I guess UMass didn't count to them), and I wanted to find out what I could accomplish at an elite program. When the Kentucky job had come open two years earlier, in 2007, I'd wanted it badly. In fact, I'd called my wife every day for, like, six days and said, "Did they call? Did they call?" Then I'd kind of figured it out: They weren't calling.

I believe that fate intervenes in life—sometimes in good ways, sometimes bad. Kentucky started playing basketball more than a century ago, in 1903, when the team competed in just three games and came away with one victory—against the Lexington YMCA. (If there had been an NCAA back then, I'm sure scheduling a game against the "Y" would have been some kind of violation.) It became a powerhouse in the Adolph Rupp years, an unbelievable run that began in 1930 and finally ended in 1972.

Joe B. Hall had the unenviable task of following his longtime boss in the job and a half dozen years later won an NCAA championship. He was followed by two big-name coaches—Eddie Sutton and Rick Pitino. But by 2009 more than a decade had passed since Kentucky's last national championship. The team had won a total of just two NCAA tournament games in the previous four seasons, and over the last two, it had lost *twenty-seven games.* That's not supposed to happen in Lexington. There was nowhere to go but up.

As the twenty-third coach in the program's history, I was following Billy Gillispie, who'd had a rough time of it, and not Tubby Smith, coach of the 1998 champions—who was still beloved and for all the right reasons. Would I have succeeded if I'd gotten the job two years earlier? Yes, I think so, but the degree of difficulty might have been a little higher.

That first day at the press conference I said that I don't walk on water and I don't have a magic wand. If anyone was hoping for something amazing to happen in just one year, I told them, I wasn't the guy they should have hired. I was hoping to buy time and patience, which I figured I might need.

But that spring we were able to quickly sign a talented class of incoming freshmen, including John Wall, DeMarcus Cousins, Eric Bledsoe, and Daniel Orton, all of whom would stay just one year before becoming first-round NBA draft picks. They joined a solid core of holdovers, including future first-round pick Patrick Patterson, and we finished with a 35-3 record and fell one game short of reaching the Final Four. The next year we made it into the Final Four, losing a close semifinal game to Connecticut. The year after that, my third at Kentucky, we were national champions. So much for lowering expectations.

Over my four seasons in Lexington, we have averaged more than thirty wins a season. An unprecedented seventeen of our players have been drafted into the NBA, thirteen in the first round. Nine were lottery picks, including two who were the top overall choices.

And it keeps on going. For the 2013–14 season we signed a class of incoming freshmen that commentators have compared to the "Fab Five," the 1991 class at Michigan led by Chris Webber and Jalen Rose. Some have said our kids are the best group of freshmen in the whole *history* of college basketball. A college basketball writer I respect said we may have *eight* NBA first-round picks on the roster. I don't pay much attention to the media stuff, but I'll say this—these young guys are good, *really* good. My guess is that at least one of them will play just ten or fifteen minutes a game and still get picked in the first round of the NBA draft.

To many college basketball fans, I'm the "one and done" guy, the coach who gets the best high school players and shuttles them off to the pros after one season. That's my reputation, but it's not the whole story. First of all, I don't like the current system—the built-in incentives for one and done; the disincentives to stay for more than one season—and I have ideas about how to fix it if the NBA, NCAA, or anyone else would listen. But right now these are the rules we play by. We *do* get more than our share of the top players at Kentucky, and in almost all cases their dream is to play in the NBA as soon as possible. The more who achieve that goal, the more who want to come here. That's the way it works. Success breeds more success. Would I be happy if we won a national championship one season and nobody got drafted? I would be happy for the program but disappointed for the kids. I wouldn't feel like I had done my job for them.

At the end of the season we sit down and talk. I don't push

players out the door, but I don't stand in their way. I tell them how they are viewed by the NBA. I've told some that it's a good idea to leave and others that they would be better off staying. They don't always do what I advise, in either direction. I've had kids decide to stay who I thought should leave. Whatever their decision, I give them a hug, tell them I love them, and promise to do everything I can to support them.

We're really good academically. Maybe that doesn't exactly square with my image as a fast-talking recruiter and, to some, a rule breaker. But it's a fact. If you come to play for me at Kentucky, you either turn pro or get a college degree—or you turn pro *and* get a degree. It's a pretty good deal.

What we do academically and what we do on the basketball court are the components of what I call our Success Rate. All ten of the players who have exhausted their eligibility in my time here have graduated. The last three seasons, our team grade point average has been better than a 3.0. (In the spring semester of 2013, it was 3.4.) We consistently place multiple players on the Southeastern Conference academic honor roll.

If you want to judge us by the NCAA's Academic Progress Rate, we had a four-year composite score of 963 last year, well above the NCAA's cutoff mark of 930. And we'll be even higher this year. (When I took over at Memphis, the team had a 0 percent graduation rate; no one, in six years, had earned a degree. Nineteen of my last twenty-two seniors graduated.)

I am not, of course, solely responsible for any of this. I've got a great staff of assistant coaches, unbelievable support in the athletic department and throughout the university. And I've benefitted from mentors, some of whom I'm still learning from.

———

What we do at Kentucky is difficult. I like to say it's *ridiculous*. It's *sick*. It's never been done before in college basketball. Guys come in, they get drafted, we bring in a new wave of players, then they move on and we have to bring in another wave. We have the turnover rate of a fast-food restaurant. The Miami Heat put together a team of superstars with LeBron and Dwyane Wade and Chris Bosh, and it took them two years to mesh and win a championship.

We have a new team every year and our fans expect championships. Big Blue Nation shows up, 24,000 strong, for every home game, and nine thousand of them stay for my postgame radio show. We could be playing Popcorn State with an ice storm pelting the whole state and you still wouldn't see an empty seat. Seats are passed on from generation to generation.

After a game, I'm looking at seventy-five reporters and fifteen cameras. I can't tell you where they all come from, but there's more media than at a Knicks game. I joke sometimes that I'm like the chairman of the Federal Reserve. People hang on my every word, and if I say something controversial—like when I said my team was "uncoachable"—it's like, *Oh my gosh, we've got to close down the borders!*

By any definition this is a big job. It's a coaching challenge, a management challenge, a human challenge. How do I teach my players all the basketball they need? How do we come together as a team and win championships? How do we forge relationships?

And it's about a lot more than basketball. Our program raises tens of millions of dollars for charity. A lot of the big stuff I do through my Web site, Twitter, and other social media. For the hands-on stuff the players come with me. At Christmastime we walk into families' apartments and homes with winter coats and presents. On days off we'll visit sick kids in hospitals. Last year I found out that Nerlens Noel, our best player, was making hospital visits on his own. He wasn't telling anybody about it but just showing up and trying to make someone's day better. That's a coaching success you won't ever see on my win-loss record—and even more so a parenting success by Nerlens's mom, Dorcina, a strong woman who came to this country from her native Haiti.

I may have some of these young men for only a season, but I ask myself, *Have I done everything I can to show them the importance of being grateful for what they have?* I say to them, "You've been blessed. That stuff you have, most of it is God given. You haven't done anything to get that body, that athleticism. So the question becomes, what are you going to do with it? Some of you are going to come across millions and millions of dollars and great fame. First you're going to help your family, but then what? How are you going to help society and your community?"

M y credo is "Players First." It drives everything I do as a coach. Notice that it's plural, not singular. Players First. We reach our personal goals by striving together toward collective goals. During the season it's all about team. After the season it's about the individual.

I made this promise on the day I became the Kentucky coach,

at the press conference. I had not even sat down with my team yet. It was not a recruiting ploy, but a statement of purpose. "As a basketball coach, I don't make a whole lot of promises. I never have," I said that day. "But we make commitments. The commitment being, this will be about Players First. I know how big this program is. But it's only big because of the players who have gone through here. This program will be about Players First. All of our staff, we're here to serve them." The fact is, that's the way I had always coached. Even in the NBA. I just had not put a name on it.

Anybody who watches me on the sideline can see how much I want to win. But I try to remember what my real job is. The Kentucky basketball program will go on and on, long after I'm gone. A hundred years from now, they'll still be playing and somebody will be coaching. One season's win-loss record won't matter. It'll be forgotten. But a year in a young man's life is not forgotten by him or his family, and it may set the trajectory for the rest of his life.

A lot of my players come out of extremely humble beginnings. Households in tough neighborhoods. Single moms with jobs that keep them on their feet all day. This is not a revelation. It's part of the known landscape of college basketball.

I ask the young men entrusted to me to dig deep within and explore what motivates them. "What is your 'why?'" I ask them. "Why are you playing basketball for the University of Kentucky, and what do you hope to achieve?"

A lot of them tell me their "why" is that they want to take care of their families. That means different things to different kids. Not every one of them is headed to the NBA. Julius Mays, a steadying influence on our turbulent 2012–13 team, memorably said, in front of all his teammates, "I'm my mother's only son, and I'm not going to fail." Other players tell me, "I'm going to take care of my mom and my grandma because they've been through so much for me. I'm going to give them the world once I make it to the league, because I promised them that."

I'll throw that right back at them. If a player is slacking off in practice, I'll say, "You said you love your mom, right?"

"Yeah, I love my mom."

"And your grandma too?"

"Yeah, I love my grandma."

"Okay, but since you're not trying very hard today, it must mean you don't love them as much today. You're not working, so it has to mean that, right?"

Honesty and its related quality, trust, are at the very core of my coaching philosophy. I'm straight up with my players from the moment I walk into their houses to recruit them. They learn that they can trust me to tell them what they need to hear—as opposed to what they may *want* to hear.

I've had kids say to me, "Can you do with me what you did with Derrick Rose?" Maybe there are coaches who would kiss the kid's behind and tell him all the ways his game is just like Derrick's, but that's not me. I say, "Are you that good? If you are, yeah. But if not, no."

None of my players are as ready as they think they are for how we play at Kentucky—let alone ready for the pros—because they have rarely if ever been really pushed. They have gotten accustomed to dominating even while putting out three-quarters effort. In fact, they probably don't even know they play at three-quarters speed. That's one of the things I have to show them.

When I went down to Texas see the Harrison twins, Andrew

and Aaron, the point guard and shooting guard on the 2013–14 team, I said to them simply, "I've seen you two be the best players in the country. You dominate, absolutely dominate, when you're challenged. But guess what? I've also seen you where you act like it doesn't matter, where you don't care. Let me tell you, those guys are not playing on my court."

It was a great moment. The twins' father, Aaron Sr., a former military man and their AAU coach, leaned toward his two sons and said, "Did you hear what he just said?"

Alex Poythress, in his freshman season, came to us as a glorious physical specimen. A beast, I called him affectionately. He's a beautiful kid, a good son, a loving brother to his twin sister, who is also a student here on campus. I think he is ultimately going to be a great player. But at first he was not living up to his potential, not even close. He didn't know how to work hard or for long enough periods of time. If I pushed him too much, he would not respond. In games we could play him only in short bursts.

Alex was having a tough time because he wanted to do better, and his teammates were having a tough time with him because they *needed* him to do better. One day after practice I had the team together in the meeting room where we watch film and talk. The room is steps away from the gym and like a small theater, with a screen and elevated rows of comfortable seats. It had been a hard practice, so everyone was sort of slumped in their chairs.

"Do you like Alex?" I asked one of the guys. "Yeah," he said, "I really like him." I went around and polled the room, asking probably a half dozen guys the same question. It was unanimous. Everybody liked Alex.

Then I turned to Alex himself, who was sitting in the second row and looking bewildered, like he wasn't sure where this was going. "You see, Alex," I said to him. "Everybody likes you. You're a great guy. They just don't like playing with you like this."

Now, maybe to some of you that sounds harsh. But I tell my players right from the beginning: "Don't come here if you want a pat on the back every day. Don't come if you want it to be easy. It's not what we do." I've already told them I'm going to keep it real. And they say, "Yeah, I like that you keep it real"—and they do, until I keep it real with them personally, and then they don't like it as much. But that's okay. I've already warned them.

You're telling me you want to be challenged? Okay, then I'm going to do that. Every single day. Playing for me is going to be the hardest thing you've ever done. If you're not up for that, go somewhere else. *Please* go somewhere else.

CHAPTER 1

MAKING LISTS, KEEPING SCORE

(LESSONS FROM MOON TOWNSHIP, PENNSYLVANIA)

'm both a hoarder and a neatnik. It's kind of a rare combination. I save a lot of stuff but I tuck it out of sight, so you won't see my desk or my dresser or any of my personal spaces cluttered with junk. The other thing I do is put things in writing. My mother was the first to tell me, if it matters to you, put it in writing. Other people said, if you really want to go after something and you're serious about it, write it down *and* give yourself a deadline.

When I was still playing in college, I made a list of objectives for the upcoming year. Two of the things on it were "get your body right" and "get closer to God." When I thought of the kind of house I'd want to live in someday, I actually drew a picture of it. I'm anal like that. It had a pool and a courtyard. I figured it was a $100,000 house, which at the time was a huge amount of money.

Not too long ago, my son, Brad, unearthed another memento, goals I wrote down when I was twenty-six years old and an assistant coach at the University of Pittsburgh. On a single sheet of paper, in neat printing, it said:

> *Become a head coach before the age of 30.*
> *Win a national championship by the fifth year.*
> *Be family oriented.*
> *Be financially secure by age 35.*
> *Make others feel good.*
> *Care about the kids.*
> *Enjoy, it's only a game!* ("Enjoy" was underlined.)
> *Continue to grow and expand with the game . . . learn*
>   *and grow.*

When I look at these goals now, I see that the ones near the top—get the big job, win a title, make money—are a young man's aspirations. Some of the others are hints of the man I hoped to become. I've met many of the objectives I set, though not all of them on the time frame I put down. (Another sign of being young: I was impatient and a little unrealistic.)

I did become a head coach by age thirty; I was twenty-nine when I took over at UMass. I won a national championship, but I don't know what I was thinking when I set out to accomplish that in five years. On the night we beat Kansas in the NCAA title game in New Orleans, I was fifty-three years old and in my twentieth season as a college coach.

I *am* financially secure, more so than I ever could have imagined. I'm not a crazy man. I don't have a lot of vices or expensive habits. So my wife, Ellen, and I believe it is important to give back to the community. We look for ways to contribute, both financially and otherwise. I have what is sometimes called walkaway money, meaning that if I ever get to a point where somebody wants me to do something I don't want to do, something I'm not comfortable with, I can say, I'm out. I'm walking. What I like most about having financial security is that Ellen and I don't ever have to talk about money. It doesn't come up. We don't argue about it. It's not a part of our lives.

The one thing on that list that is toughest to conquer is "Enjoy, it's only a game!" I'm still working on that one. Like any competitive person, and like every coach, I want to win. Not just some of the time but all the time. I want deep runs in the NCAA tournament every season, Final Four appearances, championships.

These are part of my job expectations—set from above and from within. My players want the same things, but more so than is the case for me at this point, their futures depend on it. There are a few dozen other programs and coaches out there with the same expectations and the same pressures.

What I've told myself is that I have to enjoy the anxiety. Enjoy dealing with losses. Enjoy coping with bitter disappointment, because there are millions of people who would like to be where I am, to feel what I'm feeling—even on my worst day—and they'd gladly trade places with me. So whatever's going on, however bad it feels, appreciate the fact that it's part of sports. Know that you're going to feel it, or don't do sports.

Sometimes it helps to take a step back and tell myself, *C'mon, man, you're a basketball coach! You go to work every day in a gym. In sneakers. How bad can it be?*

But I'm not always successful in keeping that perspective. Coaches have to monitor themselves, their own mental well-being. We got to where we are because of a searing competitive fire within us. It's not a normal thing, but it's who we are. Our will to win is sometimes beyond that of our players, which can be a source of frustration—or, if you let it get out of control, rage. The most intense pressure we feel is self-induced.

You bring the job home with you without even realizing that's what you're doing. My second-to-last UMass team, which won twenty-nine games and reached the Elite Eight, had a terrific shooter on it by the name of Mike Williams. He was great in the clutch and we won some games because of his last-second heroics. But he wasn't great at following team rules, and I battled with him the whole time he was with me.

I don't talk to Ellen about basketball, but I'll sometimes seek her advice when I can't figure out how to get through to a kid. I'm sure everyone in my household was also hearing me talk on the phone with my staff about the situation with Mike. When I finally had to kick him off the team late in the season, I said to my daughter Erin, "I threw Mike Williams off the team today. You're going to hear about it at school, so I just wanted you to know."

"That's good," she said.

I said, "That's good? Why's it good?"

"Because maybe now you won't talk about him so much anymore," she said.

She was *nine years old*. When stuff like that happens, you realize, *Wow, I'm totally consumed. I'm living this job day and night,*

every waking moment, and I don't even realize it. There's no sepa-
ration between this job and the other parts of my life.

Bill Parcells, the Hall of Fame football coach, gave me great advice once on how to recognize if I am still operating within a healthy range—or let's just say *healthy enough,* for my line of work. "I'll tell you when it's time to step away, Cal," he said. "I don't care what you're coaching, or where you're coaching. If winning becomes just a relief, it's time to step off the gas."

We are all, to an extent, products of where we come from. My grandfather on my father's side came from Reggio Calabria, farming country in the far south of Italy, a stone's throw across the water from Sicily. He still wasn't an American citizen when my dad was born. The work he found was in the coal mines of West Virginia, digging anthracite out of the earth from a couple of hundred feet below ground. He came out of the mine every afternoon covered in sweat and coal dust, thankful to have emerged into daylight. I look back on that and think, *How lucky am I?*

I grew up in Moon Township, Pennsylvania, outside Pittsburgh. Within Pittsburgh itself, each group still had its own part of town. The Irish lived on the north side, the Italians on the south side, the Jews in Squirrel Hill, and the blacks in what was called the Hill District. It wasn't like that in Moon Township. We were all thrown together, except that just about everybody was white. There were two black kids in my high school, and a black family lived nearby. Mostly it was straight-ahead working class. I didn't know any doctors or lawyers or other professionals. There was one guy nearby who was a teacher, and he was, like, the highest person around.

The people in my family were laborers. My mom and both my grandmothers served food in cafeterias. My dad worked at a steel mill, in the hottest, dirtiest part of the factory—the blast furnace—then got a job fueling jets at the Pittsburgh airport. After I was out of the house, the company he worked for got bought out, and he and my mom moved to North Carolina so he could work as a baggage handler. Because of various buyouts, mergers, and bankruptcies involving companies he had worked for, his pension wasn't what he thought it would be, so he ended up throwing bags until he was seventy years old.

I would never compare myself to the least fortunate of some of the kids I have coached. I always had a stable home with a mom and a dad. But in terms of wealth and material goods, I didn't come from much. There were times when my parents struggled from one Friday to the next, trying to get to the next paycheck. One of the things they always said was, "We'll never go on relief." They refused. "We'll starve, but we are not going on relief." They never had a credit card, and we never bought something we couldn't afford. We didn't go on vacations, and I was never on an airplane until I was nineteen years old.

I was the middle of three children. My two sisters slept in one of the bedrooms of our two-bedroom house and my parents slept in the other. My dad moved a wall about three or four feet and carved out a small space for me in what had been a hallway leading to the attic. I didn't have a closet but I probably didn't have enough clothes to need one. We had one bathroom, which had a tub but no shower. (It sounds funny to say now, but I didn't know anybody who took showers. Everybody took baths.)

One of the best things about our house was its location—right across the street from the high school. After I became well-known as a coach, our old athletic director would tell stories of how I had a set of keys to the gym. I didn't, but I can understand how it seemed that way.

The school had doors that could be propped open. You just sort of had to jerk them. They didn't want to change all the doors, so they put chains on them to keep them from opening all the way. I was really skinny, 150 pounds when I graduated from high school, so all I had to do was get my head through the little space and I could squeeze my body in. I was like a rat contorting my frame through a small opening—almost literally a gym rat.

Eventually they put big floor-to-ceiling metal gates in the hallways, so even if somebody got in they couldn't easily travel around the school. But I found a way around that too. I'd go through the auditorium, which had a door that let you out right in front of the gym. It was pitch dark in there, so I felt my way along the walls.

Weekends, holidays, just about every chance I got I was in that gym working on my game. I'd take shots from different parts of the floor, practice foul shots, work on my ball handling. I wrote down everything I did. I tell my guys now: "You've got to love the grind." That's something they probably hear from me more than anything else. *You've got to love the grind.* Embrace the work. Embrace the sweat. Embrace the pain.

And keep track of it all, because it keeps you honest. You've got to chart a workout and chart your shots. If there's not something measurable, it's not real. You say to yourself, *I'm taking five hundred shots before I leave this gym, and I'm doing it every day.* Count them up and write down how many you made.

And if you miss a day, write that down too, so you can look back on that and feel bad about it. You didn't hit a big foul shot at the end of the game? You clanked a jumper off the back rim that would've tied the game? Look in your workout book. Maybe that's because of the days you slacked off.

I played every sport when I was a kid, but I'm not a person wired to stand out in center field, hoping somebody hits me a fly ball every couple of innings. My mind races too fast for that. I fell in love with the speed of basketball—not just how fast the game can be played but also how quickly you can improve your skills if you're willing to spend time.

You learn three or four moves, you practice them, and it can happen fast if you really zero in on it. I enjoyed going to the gym by myself. I enjoyed going in with one other guy. I loved making myself better. I liked it as much as the prize.

There's no instant gratification in basketball, but you can sense yourself getting better. You build your own self-esteem, your self-control, your self-confidence. I tell my players: "You don't need me praising you. You can see your own improvement." Now, you've got to transfer it all into the game, but the grind helps you. And when you see the results, it drives you right back to the gym. You want to grind even harder.

As a coach I don't miss practices. I just don't. I'll go out on the road twenty-five or thirty times during a season to recruit and still not miss one day on the court with our team. Somebody will argue that I recruit the whole year, so how's that possible? But I recruit on off days, or I fly out after our practice to see a high school kid and I'm back in time for our next practice the following afternoon. (This is a big advantage of coaching at a school like Kentucky; the revenue we generate allows me to fly by private plane when needed.)

I want my players to know that I, as their coach, love the grind of practices. For me they are much more fun than the tests we have to take at the games. Those become a chess match with the other coach, which I enjoy, but not as much as watching my team grow on the practice court.

In the NBA the skill that scouts consider least, when evaluating talent, is shooting. Think about that. It's an essential component, obviously—the only way to put points on the board. But anybody who wants to work at shooting a basketball can get better if they dedicate themselves to it. Michael Jordan didn't shoot great when he was younger. Neither did Magic. But they became great clutch shooters.

When I was with the Nets, we brought in Tracy McGrady, whom we were thinking about drafting, for two workouts. I'm not kidding when I say he didn't make more than five shots. He was one of the worst shooters I had ever seen. He barely made free throws. We brought him back a second time because we couldn't believe how many he missed, and he was the same. So I passed on him. Five years later, I'm watching him on TV, and he's knocking everything down—if he's open, *boom,* he hits it. That's what happens if you dedicate yourself. The point is that you can improve individual skills if you're willing to spend time. It's almost guaranteed. And *until* a player improves, he can compensate with his athleticism and his devotion to facets of the game like defense, rebounding, and playmaking.

Contrast that with, say, baseball, where a player might have every single thing going for him except that he can't hit a curveball—and he might spend six long years in the minor leagues trying to figure out how to hit that pitch. And if he can't, he just dies on the vine. He never has a career. There's no equivalent to that in our sport. If you've got the talent inside you, it's fully within your power to nurture it. Almost every kid I bring in has NBA-caliber athleticism. More than anything, that's what I try to get across to them: You control your own destiny. It's up to you.

There are players in the NBA who don't love the grind and don't love playing—they're just doing it because they're supposed to and it's a way of making money—but they don't last and they're never special. They may make it for a while and be nice NBA players, but they'll be forgotten about the moment they leave the game.

I see it with my own players who go into the league. How are they going to be after they get their first checks? Is that enough for them, or is their goal to be special? That's what it comes down to. I've sent a couple of players into the NBA who I sometimes fear are just happy to be there, but most of them, I'm happy to say, have kept on working to make themselves better.

Talent is not the determining thing; grit is. To give one example, Brandon Knight has a drive to be the best. He doesn't have the ideal physical frame, but he will max out because he'll never quit grinding. The guys who love the grind—the Kobes, the Michaels, the Larry Birds—they come an hour and a half before everybody else and get the ball boys to rebound for them. They're never satisfied.

In the summer before my senior year of high school, my friends and I started traveling together and looking for pickup basketball games all around Pittsburgh. We'd all pile into one car and go to different playgrounds, because that's how you did it in those days. There was no AAU.

I was the one who would get everyone together. I'd call the guys and say, "Let's go into the city," or to Monaca, one of the nearby towns. Or "Let's go to Midland, and if there are no ballgames there, we'll head to Aliquippa." And we did that all summer, five or six of us in the car—the core of the team for that upcoming season.

Back then I would sometimes say something stupid to a kid that didn't need to be said—some insult or comeback when I would have been better off just walking away. It was normal immaturity. I was type A, but not the kind of kid who's an irritant. Maybe I still rub some people the wrong way. But I wasn't a habitual punk or wiseass; I was a gatherer, the same way I see myself now. If I'm in New York, I'm having dinner with twelve people and they're all friends of mine. At the Final Four, we have a dinner every year—guys I used to coach with, friends from various stops—and there are at least forty of us.

Basketball is an intimate sport. Think about some of the words we use. *Sharing* the ball. *Sacrificing* for teammates. *Helping* on defense. It's the same words you use in relation to a family. It's all about shared responsibility. You've got just five players on the court at the same time. You don't have seventy-eight guys on a roster—offense, defense, special teams—you've got a dozen. We all know one another. We've all got to live together.

Character matters probably a little more than it does in other sports. Kenny Payne, one of my assistant coaches, uses the term "teamsmanship"—which is like citizenship in a basketball context. Play the game the right way. Care about one another. Keep the commitments you've made to your teammates.

I like to say that you probably won't succeed if you've got jagoffs on your team, and if your best player is a jagoff, you've got absolutely *no* chance. Okay, I know that sounds like a bad word, but it's not what you think. It's a word particular to Pittsburgh and western Pennsylvania. (If you don't believe me, look it up on the Internet under "Pittsburghese.") A jagoff is someone who is a jerk or a loudmouth. He's selfish. He probably doesn't pull his weight on the job. He's a guy you don't want to be around.

I heard stories about my grandfather and the men he worked with in the mines. They'd be joking around before they went down into the shaft, and at the end of the shift they'd go out for a couple of beers and tell more jokes. But underground it was all business. They had one another's backs. If even one guy was a jagoff, it put everybody else in danger. It's the same with a basketball team. We're all business on the court. In the locker room we're laughing all the time. We're throwing stuff at one another. Guys leave the practice facility in groups of three and four— never alone. I've yet to be around a successful basketball team that was grim and humorless or where guys went their own separate ways.

I was a good but not great high school player—an inch short of six feet tall, sort of fast but not superathletic. I was a point guard, like so many future coaches. I could shoot the ball but I liked passing it better. I learned the value of *team* back in Moon Township—what could be accomplished by a group of players who are in harmony. We went to the Western Pennsylvania play-offs in my senior year, the first time my school had qualified in thirty years. We would never have accomplished that if it hadn't been for the time we'd spent playing together and bonding the previous summer. We were also fortunate to play for a coach, Bill Sacco, who cared for us and was a great role model.

I left Moon Township to play college ball at North Carolina–Wilmington, a Division I program, but didn't get much playing time. I don't think I got treated badly, but it was disappointing. Halfway through my sophomore season, I transferred to Clarion State, a Division II school in Pennsylvania that had recruited me out of high school. It was a good experience because I got to play. The coach, Joe DeGregorio, was a master motivator, and I've always been grateful to him for taking me in. (In my senior season I achieved a rare statistical feat—averaging 5.3 points a game and 5.3 assists.)

I don't bring much of my playing career forward into my coaching career, or at least I don't think I do. It was a whole different level, a different time, so there's no big reason to look back on it. As a player I had absolutely nothing in common with a Derrick Rose, an Eric Bledsoe, or some of the other point guards I've been privileged to coach.

But my wife thinks my own playing experiences taught me, as she puts it, "how to be fair to players." Nothing was ever handed to me, and I never got anything based on my reputation, because outside of Moon Township I didn't have one. I worked for every single thing I got. A lot of the kids I bring in to play at Kentucky are nationally known before they even arrive, but I throw the

whole competition open from day one. No one is promised playing time. They're not promised anything except an opportunity.

When you grow up in close quarters like I did, I think you
can go one of two ways. You can become the type of
person who, if you get some money, buys a big house out in the
country where you can't see any neighbors. It's quiet. Maybe
you've got horses, stables, a long driveway, and big iron gates. I
don't know what else, maybe a private lake and a putting green.
Your own airstrip. You never have to worry about interacting
with someone outside your family or chosen circle of friends.

Or you stay what you were—a person who is used to a lot of
human contact and likes it. You don't run away from other people; you gravitate to them.

In my first coaching job we didn't live close enough to the
UMass campus in Amherst because we couldn't afford it. I hated
it. I used to say we lived up on the mountain. I left in the morning when it was dark, and when I got home it was dark. If I
wanted to come home for lunch, the round trip, with traffic and
stoplights, could end up taking me an hour and a half. It wasn't
always easy to have my players around the house because of the
distance. But we did it anyway. At that point in our lives, I don't
know if we did it more for the players, or for Ellen and me.

When I took the job at Memphis, I said to Ellen, "We're not
doing it that way again." We bought a house right across the
street from campus. In Lexington we live right in town. It's a
generous-sized house, nothing like Moon Township, but it's on

a main street and no more than a five-minute drive from the University of Kentucky campus.

In the mornings, on my way from Mass to my office, I stop at a Dunkin' Donuts for a cup of coffee. Anybody who wants to wish me luck on an upcoming game, ask a question about strategy, or suggest a lineup change can come up to me and say hello—and plenty of people do. I don't consider it an imposition. If I felt that way, I would have my coffee at home.

In the middle of the day I'll stop back at the house and have a quick sandwich or salad with Ellen, whom I met in my first assistant-coaching job at Kansas. She was working in the business office. We don't talk a lot about basketball, but she keeps an eye on my demeanor on the sideline and how I am with particular kids.

After a game she might say something like "Quit yelling at DeMarcus so much." Actually, she *did* say exactly that once. She loved DeMarcus Cousins.

"What, you're going to tell me how to coach now?" I replied.

"You're yelling at him all the time, but the other guys are doing stuff wrong too. Go yell at them."

I'm sure she was right.

Ellen meets the players for the first time when I'm recruiting them and they come with their families to our house for dinner. She bakes each of them brownies on their birthdays. She becomes a quasi-mother. If it's been too long since I've had them at the house, she gets mad at me and says, "When are you bringing the guys over here?"

We had a player come to Kentucky who had been at another school, and he told Ellen and me he had never been inside the coach's house. We were like, "What? You've never been over there?" That may be the norm, but our kids are in the house a lot—especially early in the season, when we're having two practices a day. I like having them over for an occasional meal so I know they're getting enough to eat.

It's the same thing when classes are not in session over the holidays and we stay on campus to practice—a grueling time that is sometimes referred to as "Camp Cal." They're worn out. They come to the house in the middle of the day and I tell them they have to take naps. They spread out all over the house—the basement, whatever couch they can find, spare bedrooms. You look around the house and see a huge kid sprawled out in every room, dead asleep.

But having them at the house is not just about rest and nutrition. I like them to see how I am with my wife and kids, and I don't say that to imply that I am some kind of paragon of a family man. But I'm a successful guy who makes a good living—just as many of them will—and at the same time, I'm not a god in my own household. Just the opposite. My kids tease me, like any other dad gets teased. My daughter Erin now zings me on her Twitter feed. I go out in the backyard and pick up the dogs' poop.

People talk about the "intensity" of coaching, as if it were all about watching films, drawing up plays, yelling at refs. For me those things are only part of it—and in the ways that truly matter, they're secondary.

If I see one of my players on campus, in the hallways of the practice facility, I'll never walk by him. I'll grab him. I'll touch him. "What's happening?" "Where are you going?" "Did you talk to your mom today?"

There's not a coach time and a not-coach time. I'm always their coach. If I just walk away, or I look too busy or preoccupied, they don't know, as a seventeen-year-old or eighteen-year-old, what that means. They wonder, *Why did he do that?* I don't want them to think for a moment that I don't care about them. I don't want them to have a second's worth of doubt.

I made another list after the 2012–13 season, which was a particularly bad year for us, one of my worst ever in coaching. It was to remind myself of what my job really is—its meaning and higher purpose. This is what I wrote.

> *NURTURER: That's what I am. Be patient and create*
> *a successful environment.*
> *PROTECTOR: Help guard them against themselves*
> *and others.*
> *CHALLENGER: Help them push through comfort*
> *levels. Make them uncomfortable.*
> *TEACHER: Help them create within themselves a love*
> *of learning and growth.*
> *PROMOTER: Put them on a stage. If we lose, it's on*
> *me. If we win, they get all the glory. Players First.*
> *LASTLY, A FATHER: Give them unconditional love at*
> *all times.*

If I can come close to doing these six things, the rest will take care of itself. As a coach, things come at you that are beyond basketball. You're not specifically trained for them unless you have a degree in counseling, which I don't. You just hope your life experience prepares you to handle them.

When I was the coach at Memphis, I had a player who had never met his father. That's not a common thing on my teams, but it's not unheard of, either. I've had other kids in that same situation.

We were about to go up to play a game in New York at Madison Square Garden. He took me aside and said that his dad had been in contact and wanted to meet him when we came into the city. The father told him he had spent some years in prison, but now he was a changed man and had some kind of ministry in New York. This kid's mom hated the dad, so he didn't know what to do. Would it be disloyal to agree to a meeting?

I told him that I couldn't make a decision for him, but if he refused to meet with his father, it would be irrevocable. It would be an opportunity lost, and he might regret it. If he had the meeting, he could ask his father why he had chosen to be absent. Even if he was in prison, why didn't he ever write a letter or call on the telephone if he could?

So he decided to meet him, and they arranged a time and a place. The young man went to where they were supposed to get together, and the father never showed up. I saw the kid later that day and he was in tears. He was nineteen years old, and it was as if he'd been deserted all over again. It was heartbreaking.

All I could say was, "You did everything right. It's your father's loss. You just have to try to remember that. You gave him a chance. He had an opportunity to meet his son, to see what a great young man you are, and he blew it."

If we lose a game, I don't sleep well. Was it my fault? Could I have done something differently and we would have won? Something like this puts your life and work in perspective. You look back and hope you gave good advice, that your words of comfort were the right words.

Ardent Kentucky basketball fans probably remember my contretemps with Josh Harrellson in 2010. Josh was there when I arrived—a really big kid, six foot eleven, fleshy, pushing three hundred pounds.

I didn't dislike him, but he could drive me nuts. He wasn't in great shape. He liked to clown around in practice and make everybody laugh. Josh didn't play my first year, but at the start of my second season—his senior year—he got twenty-plus rebounds, a big number, in the Blue-White Scrimmage.

Fine, but he was matched up against Eloy Vargas. Josh had at least forty pounds on Eloy. When the press asked me after the game about Josh's performance, I said, "Can he do this for fifteen, twenty minutes a game? If he can go in there and grab rebounds, then do it. Either we're the worst defensive rebounding team in America or he's gotten better, one of the two. I haven't figured it out. We'll watch the tape and figure it out."

Josh decided he had to answer me. On Twitter. "Just amazing I can't get a 'good job' or a 'way to go,'" he tweeted. Later he tweeted his displeasure at not being featured on our Big Blue Madness poster.

He deleted the tweet quickly, but someone grabbed it and it was out there. People were talking about it. When I saw it, I was pissed off, probably a little more than I should have been. But it was a scrimmage, not a real game. How excited was I supposed to get about it? We've got six months and about forty games left to play, and he wants to take a victory lap? And then he takes a shot at me on Twitter?

My first thought was *It's the last straw, and I've finally had it with him. I'm throwing him off the team.* Even though Ellen thought I should give him another chance.

He knew I was irritated and wanted to explain himself, but I wouldn't take his call. I was going to make this dude sweat for as many days as I could, okay? So for two days I didn't talk to him. The staff told him they didn't know if he was on the team or off.

I really was ready to kick him off the team. I figured we might be better off without him. Then I woke up one morning, went to Mass, and thought to myself, *How would I want my own son to be treated? You have to give this young man another chance.* It just took that one moment, away from all the rest of the noise, to lead me to do the right thing.

I thought, *I don't want to cost him his career. If he doesn't change, he'll do that to himself, but I have to open the door and let him back in.* We usually only practice two hours a day, so there's plenty of time for individual sessions. That day, I say to Josh, "Here's the deal. You're going to come in for thirty minutes before every practice and do conditioning with Kenny. He's going to kick your ass and you're going to get in the best shape of your life. If you can't tolerate it, you can quit, but that's on you."

He did his sessions with Kenny. Some nights he came back in at eleven o'clock at night and worked out on his own. He ended up helping lead us to the Final Four. After that season he got drafted in the second round and made the New York Knicks roster. Since that time he's played for the Miami Heat and a couple of teams overseas before starring in China. He signed a guaranteed deal in the off-season to be a backup center for the Detroit Pistons. I'm sure he's already made a million dollars playing basketball. He's not going to be a star anywhere, but if he works at it, he can be a solid NBA veteran. I will always err in a kid's favor—if they do sort of goofy stuff like Josh, or sometimes if they do worse. Sometimes fans think: *How did you let a kid get away with such and such? Why wouldn't you kick him off the team?* You sometimes have to battle a college president or athletic director over these situations. It also taught me that some kids need to be treated differently.

But I'm not going to throw a kid under the bus to satisfy somebody else. And I never believe that if a player makes a mistake, it's a reflection on me. It's only a reflection on me if I do the same stupid stuff they do. Now, if they don't change, that *does* become a reflection on what I accept. It's a fine line, like so many things in coaching, but if I'm serious about the philosophy of Players First, I have to care more about their future than about what people might think of me.

I realize I've mentioned my faith several times already. My spiritual beliefs are not the point of this book, and I don't come from a religious tradition that calls upon me to try to bring others to my way of thinking. For me, spirituality is mostly a private thing. But I do want to explain it in a little more detail, because what I believe is such a critical part of how I coach.

I grew up Catholic. We went to church on Sundays, but nobody went to Mass every day, and it is not something I began doing until fairly recently. It began with my reading a book by Vince Lombardi, who went to Mass every morning. (Lombardi at one point was going to be a priest; I was never in danger of that.) I found out that another coach I looked up to, Don Shula, also went to Mass every morning. I read a book by Edward Bennett Williams, a big Washington lawyer who owned the Redskins, who did the same thing. I figured that there must be something to this. These people had all-encompassing jobs, but they set time aside and they did it every day.

I started going to daily Mass when I was in Memphis and continued it in Lexington—usually the 8:00 A.M. Mass at Christ the King church. Right away I liked the routine of it. I guess you could say it is its own grind, but in a very different way. It establishes a daily time to be quiet, to close out the noise, to think about what truly matters.

In church I may pray for God to give me strength, courage, the ability to deal with whatever the day may bring, but my prayers are mainly for all the other people in my life—my family, my players, my past players, my secretary, other people on my staff. If I have to tell a player he is no longer a part of our team because his presence is not helping the others, which has happened very rarely, I'll say in a prayer, *I've let go of your hand*, and ask God to take care of that person. I light candles for people who are sick. If somebody I know is having a problem, I say, "I'll pray for you." I write the names down, and I say prayers for them at Mass the next morning.

Everyone has setbacks. I don't ask God to give me an easy ride through life or nothing but success. When I was coaching Memphis, we lost a national championship game to Kansas after it seemed like we had it won. We were up nine points with two minutes and twelve seconds to play. If you replayed those last two minutes another hundred times, we'd win it ninety-nine of them. It shouldn't have happened, but it did.

As we were losing our lead, there was a time-out, one of those that go on for two minutes. I talked to the team. Before they went back out on the court, I stepped away for a moment and said a silent prayer. *God, whatever your will, I will accept. I'll deal with it.* I didn't want to *have* to deal with losing, but the strength I gained from my faith allowed me after the game to support and comfort my players. It allowed me to be a Players First coach—to take care of *their* feelings and *their* pain, not my own.

I'm not hung up on a particular religion or denomination. My wife is a Methodist and we have raised our children that way because at the time, she was more of a Methodist than I was a Catholic. We've had our kids in Christian schools. The traditions are a little different. The language that's used isn't what I grew up with. At one school that we considered for our daughter, the head of the school asked me if I had been baptized and I said that I had been. And then he asked, "What is your testimony?" And I just looked at him and said, "I don't have one. I'm Catholic. My testimony is 'I didn't do it.'"

My team knows I go to Mass every day. I tell them I pray for them, but other than that I don't talk about it. I'm at a public university. It wouldn't be appropriate. Some of the players have their own chapel service on game days, but I don't go to it. That's their thing, and I don't ever want anyone to feel pressured because of what I do.

But I do believe that anybody is helped if they have a belief in a higher power. I don't know how you get through life without that. As I wrote earlier, I would never complain about the burdens of my job because I am so fortunate to have this position. But it's a pressure-packed, competitive profession. I'm responsible for a dozen or so young men and, at the same time, I'm essentially the CEO of a pretty big business. Kentucky basketball produces annual revenues of $35 million to $40 million.

My faith helps me keep things in perspective—and it keeps my worst instincts in check. As a coach, you're trying to get kids to do things they don't naturally want to do. You're trying to get them out of their comfort level. You're challenging them, pushing them. You can feel like you're in a battle with them. I say to myself: *My will is always going to be stronger than theirs.*

There's an expression you hear sometimes: "hard coaching." I can't say what it means exactly. It might mean different things to different people. It may refer to coaching tactics that go right to the edge of what is acceptable. And guys sometimes go over that line—good coaches and good men who have lapses in judgment. I don't defend them, but I understand how it can happen.

I like to think that one of the things my faith does is keep me on the right side of that line. Nothing I need to get across on my practice court is important enough to violate a young man's human dignity.

It also helps that my practices are open, which keeps a coach in check. At UMass anybody could walk in off the street. At Memphis the press could observe. We can't be as open at Kentucky because we'd have thousands of people in there—you have to have prior approval—but we always have at least a dozen people sitting along the wall, including kids.

Basketball coaches, for whatever reason, tend to be extremely profane with their teams. It's ingrained in the culture. The perception of me is probably that every other word is an F-bomb, but it's not true. I slip up sometimes, and when I get called on it, I try to fix it.

In Memphis I had a bunch of guys I talked with at the dough-nut shop in the morning, including my friend Coach David. He called me after a Memphis game he watched on TV and I said, "What's up, Coach David?"

He said, "Cal, I can read your lips. You can't do that. You got kids watching."

I said, "Coach, I apologize."

One last thing about faith and how it helps keep me bal-anced. College coaching is rife with jealousy. Why is it like that? It's not that way in the NBA. I don't think college football is as bad as we are. Instead of lifting one another up, we've got coaches who want to tear the other guy down. It's absolutely the worst thing about the business. I have jealous impulses myself. I do what I can to keep them in check. If I'm watching a game and start to root for a certain coach to lose, I turn off the TV. I don't want to be that way.

Why would another coach feed stuff to an NCAA investigator, without regard for whether it's even true? My belief is that cer-tain people can't get up on top of the ladder on their own, so they want to drag somebody else down. Has someone done that to me? Sometimes I feel that way, but I can't tell you for certain. You have rivalries that ripen into ancient feuds and you can't even remember how they started. I've had stuff that happened in my life where I put some people on the shelf, didn't talk to them anymore, and then looked back and said, *What's that about? Every time I see this guy I'm mad, but what am I mad about?* As anyone who has been in the public eye as long as I have knows, there comes a point where you can't hurt me. You really can't. But if you're determined and dishonest enough, you can hurt the people around me. There are things that I wish I weren't, but I am. I don't need to be that way, especially at my age. The urge to sin through pride, jealousy, ego, and envy exists in me—and is a daily battle. That's why I say I'm a sinner. I know what I am. You want to know why faith is important to me? Because it's the only thing that keeps me from strangling some dudes.

It's not right for me to even have that in my heart. So I sit in Mass every morning and I think about stuff. The guy who tries to stab you—you're supposed to say, "Look, I forgive you," and then you move on. That's what you're taught.

CHAPTER 2

JUST TWO WORDS

Sports slogans are as old as sport itself. The ancient Greeks, whose original Olympic Games date back to 776 BC, are credited with the phrase "a healthy mind in a healthy body." (Some know the words in Latin—*mensana in corpore sano*.) The current Olympic motto—"higher, swifter, stronger"—is attributed to Pierre de Coubertin, the inventor of the modern Olympic Games, though he's said to have lifted the words from a French priest who organized footraces and other athletic competitions at his country school.

Vince Lombardi said, "Winning isn't everything, it's the only thing." Al Davis, the late owner of the Oakland Raiders, updated that to the hipper-sounding "Just win, baby." When I coached at UMass, our motto was "Refuse to Lose."

What all of these slogans have in common is that they are directed at the athletes and meant to inspire them to heroic feats—or to forge a collective will among competitors in team sports so they will settle for nothing less than victory. They are rallying cries.

"Players First" is a different kind of motto. It has meaning for our players, but mostly it is a watchword for me, for my assistant coaches, and for everyone else connected with Kentucky basketball. It reminds us of what our program is all about, and it influences every single thing we do—from recruiting to our style of play to my interactions with the NCAA to the amenities in our basketball facilities and locker rooms to a hundred other things.

There was a point in my life when I said to myself, *Okay, you're trying to pull yourself up in this profession that you've chosen. You're trying to grab on to something and survive, and it's not easy.* There was no epiphany that changed that. No flash, no revelation. But as I became more secure, I liked that I could make my life about everyone but me—my players, their families, my family, my assistant coaches, my secretary, my staff, people in the community.

I still make demands on players. I make *more* demands than I ever have—and tougher ones. But I'm not asking for *me*. My personal gain is off the table, a nonfactor.

Players First starts from the moment I recruit a player. I'll say, "I'm good, my family is good. The program is good. So use me. Use me for everything I know, everybody I know, every ounce of knowledge that I have about this game or anything else."

When I talk to recruits, I tell them what I saw in their game, where they need to go with it, what they need to add. If they have bad body language, I let them know, because in the rarefied world they inhabit, there's a good chance nobody else has ever pointed it out. I just say, "Hey, maybe you don't realize it, but you're putting out a message that isn't good for you. It might not be hurting you now, but it will if you don't change it."

Whether or not that player ultimately comes with me, I want to have had some kind of impact, something he got from me that helps him or his family.

When kids do choose our program, there is another phrase they hear from me: "servant leadership." The phrase was coined by a man named Robert Greenleaf, an executive for AT&T who in 1970 wrote an essay titled "The Servant as Leader"—then spent the last two decades of his life lecturing around the world on his management philosophy and at the Center for Servant Leadership, which he founded in his native state of Indiana. (It was originally called the Center for Applied Ethics.)

The underpinning of his philosophy could not be simpler: Institutions serve people, not the other way around. So as a servant-leader, I measure my success by the success of those whom I'm serving. And I model my own behavior in order to create servant-leaders among my players.

Greenleaf wrote: "The servant-leader is a servant first. . . . It begins with the natural feeling that one wants to serve, to serve *first*. Then conscious choice brings one to aspire to lead. That person is sharply different from one who is *leader* first, perhaps because of the need to assuage an unusual power drive or to acquire material possessions. . . .

"The difference manifests itself in the care taken by the servant-first to make sure that other people's highest priority needs are being served. The best test, and difficult to administer, is: Do those served grow as persons? Do they, *while being served*, become healthier, wiser, freer, more autonomous, more likely themselves to become servants?"

As you read this, you might be thinking: *Really? Many of the kids you coach are teenagers, the most selfish age, and they're not even remotely normal teenagers. When they announce they're coming to Kentucky, they hold press conferences in their high school gyms, often with the school band and cheerleaders and the whole student body in attendance. ESPN carries it live. They're that special, and they know it, because people have been telling them so since they first had a basketball in their hands. And you are going to turn them into selfless beings—something called servant-leaders?*

Yes, it's possible. I've seen it.

Most of the people reading this book will probably be familiar with our 2011–12 national championship team, or at least the broad outlines of it. We won thirty-eight games. We went 18-0 at home and 16-0 in the Southeastern Conference. We defeated Kansas in the national championship game at the Superdome in New Orleans. Six of our players were drafted that June into the NBA—four of them in the first round.

But there is something else that stays with me from that season, a true measure of who we were. I hold it dear because it demonstrates what I'm about, what our program is about, and what I want our kids to be about. Anthony Davis and Michael Kidd-Gilchrist—who a couple of months after the championship game become the number one and number two picks in the NBA draft, the first time players from the same school were the top two choices—took the fourth- and fifth-most shots on our team that season. They were the best players in college basketball, in the judgment of the NBA, and they deferred to others and let them have more of what are presumed to be the most precious commodities in basketball: shots and points.

You think those two weren't servant-leaders? Anthony and

Michael didn't care about their personal glory. They didn't care about shots and points. They totally got that Players First is *plural*. All they cared about—and cared *deeply* about—was their team and teammates.

That kind of team play comes from closeness and truly caring about other people. The guys have to love to play together, and they have to love being together. As men we don't tell each other that. We don't say, "I really like you," "Here's specifically what I like," or "Here's why I feel better about myself when we're hanging out together."

But one of the great things about basketball is that with teams that are really special, you can see those feelings expressed on the court. During that season, Anthony and Michael took a huge step toward achieving their personal goals, and they were richly rewarded for it—in large part, I'd say, because the NBA values what they valued. Selflessness. And at the same time they lifted up everyone around them.

The art of coaching at this level is about convincing great athletes to change. First we have to get them to accept what they're not good at. My assistant coaches and I use the word "surrender." Surrender to our instruction. Surrender to physical conditioning. If you're delusional and see yourself one way while the rest of the world sees something else, let it go. Believe what we're telling you.

Players arrive here from a culture in which they have played mostly for themselves. They've always had their eye on the next step up the ladder and the one above that. Lots of times they've been coddled by family members or by a coach or by people around them. Some of them come into college basketball believing that they have to get a certain number of minutes and shots. They're entitled. They feel it's owed to them.

I've won more than five hundred college games and coached thirty players who went on to play in the NBA. I coached in the league myself. I evaluated players and I drafted them. I know what happens in the predraft workouts and what's on the psychological tests the NBA gives to players.

You want to know what delusional is? I've had to say to kids: "You're listening to your barber instead of listening to me. Does that really make sense? When we play, you're showing off what you want to show and not what they want to see. As a matter of fact, you're showing them stuff that's hurting you. I keep telling you that, but you still do it."

There is no daylight whatsoever between a style of individual play that helps us win games at Kentucky and a style that will impress the NBA. *None.* That's one of the points I make repeatedly. Be in the present. Play for us. Nothing you do that helps us lose will impress them. So will you listen? Will you let me define your game?

Sometimes a player will say, "You just don't understand my game." But we do. Believe me, we get it. We're just not liking it.

Improvement is not just about working harder. If you're a drug addict and you work harder without recognizing what your problem is, then what are you—a better drug addict? You've got to admit to a bunch of people what your problem is and then figure out how to change it.

A great example of a player who surrendered and helped us and himself is Marquis Teague, the freshman point guard on our

2011–12 team. I'm going to write in much more detail about that championship team in a later chapter, but before I do, I want to tell you about Marquis, because he illustrates what can happen when a gifted player allows us to coach him.

Marquis was a good kid with a strong sense of himself. On the court he was a killer, about six foot two but absolutely physical through his body. He could get to the rim and was a great layup shooter.

When Marquis chose to come with us, he was following in a line of point guards who had played for me in recent years, at both Kentucky and Memphis, who became first-round draft picks— Derrick Rose, Tyreke Evans, John Wall, Eric Bledsoe, and Brandon Knight.

There are NBA superstars and future superstars in that group. Derrick was Rookie of the Year in 2009 and MVP in 2011, and in 2010 Tyreke was Rookie of the Year. Anyone playing point guard for me is going to be compared to them, so it takes a confident young man to step into the job. In addition, Marquis's brother, Jeff, was already playing point guard in the NBA, so he had that legacy to follow.

I saw him for the first time at the LeBron James Skills Academy in Cleveland, a big event for top high school players. He was a rising junior, playing on a middle court, and I was sitting there watching him with LeBron. Every decision he made was a good decision. Marquis was a tough, hard-nosed, loosey-goosey athlete with a live body. He had that ultimate competitive way about him, like he would fight you if he had to. I fell in love with him right away.

Later I found out his dad had played for Rick Pitino at Boston University. And his brother Jeff had played at Wake Forest, but

Jeff told him, "You need to go with Calipari. You want to be a pro; that's what he does."

But not everybody was sold on Marquis. I was told when I first recruited him: "You'll never win with him as your point guard. He didn't win in high school, he shoots too much, he's not into his team, he has a body language that doesn't bespeak a champion." I didn't believe any of it.

But in the beginning of his freshman season, his first and only one at Kentucky, he wasn't giving us what we needed. It wasn't because he was stubborn or inherently selfish or because he was listening to people from back home. He just wasn't getting it yet. I couldn't get him out of his comfort zone—which was to rely on his athleticism, put his head down, and drive the ball all the way to the hoop. That worked every time in high school, but now he was going up against opponents who could challenge him physically. He had to pick his spots.

I want a point guard who can score, but he was looking too much for his own shot and not enough to his teammates. The fans could see it and there was talk on the radio and in the blogs about replacing him with Doron Lamb, who was our shooting guard. Doron wasn't a natural at the point, but he could play it, and it became like a mantra: *Put Doron at the point. We're better with Doron at the point.* I could not care less what people said, but I knew Marquis heard the talk.

I wrote earlier that honesty—by which I mean straight talk—is the essential element of Players First. I'll extend that thought a little further. If you BS your players, you'll get that in return. But when a coach is direct with players, it leads them, in time, into making honest self-appraisals. And when they reach a point when they say they want to change, they are more likely to really mean it. It won't be just empty words.

Marquis came into my office in December of that year, after the Indiana game, which was one of our only two losses. He knew he was flailing around and standing in the way of our progressing as a team. He said, "Coach, tell me how to get better."

We had talked about all of this already, of course, but now he was approaching me, away from his teammates, and acknowledging that he had come to a crossroads. It was time for him to take a step in an affirmative direction or we might have to move on with him in a reduced role. (Our fans may be, as I said, crazy, but they know basketball. They could see that there were times Doron was giving us better minutes at the point.)

I said, "You're not doing what we're asking you to do; you're doing what you want to do. You can't be that way at that position."

There's such a fine balance to point-guard play. The player at that position is the on-court manifestation of a servant-leader. His own needs come last. And yet at the same time there are moments in a game—and even within offensive possessions, when the shot clock is winding down—that he must absolutely dominate. I don't recruit point guards if all they can do is skitter around the perimeter, pass the ball, and get out of the way. That's not enough for me.

They need to be dynamic but nuanced—able to play at different speeds and with varying levels of aggression. Other positions aren't like that. If you've got a six-foot-nine, 250-pound power forward with springs in his legs, you say to him, "Here's your job: Go after every rebound."

I had to get Derrick to score more. I had to get Tyreke to score less. I said to Marquis that this stuff isn't easy, especially for a freshman entrusted with leading a team that faced the expectations that had been put on our group. But for us to take the next step, he had to grasp it. "I want you to score to keep the defense honest," I told him that day. "That's the whole thing. If they don't play you, you have the ultimate green light. If it's in transition and you can get to the rim, you do it every time. But in every other situation, you're playing first for us, then to score, not the other way around."

As he was leaving, I said, "I'm going to work with you every day. You're my point guard, and I'm with you. I don't care what anybody says, I'm not changing that."

I don't have a "system" that we run year after year at Kentucky. I'm not that guy walking around the rail yard, inspecting the machinery, retreating into the office to look at spread sheets. *Yep, everything is in working order. We're leaving and arriving at the right times. It all looks good. The system is just how I want it!*

I'm all about the passengers, the people inside. What's it like for them?

We're not a team that always runs the motion offense or the high-low offense. We don't full-court press on every possession, and we don't play zone defense all of the time or none of the time. We do what fits the players we have.

Sometimes I think a system is an extension of a coach's ego—you know, like, *This is what we have to do, no matter whom we've got, because I invented it and I perfected it.* I don't mean to be overly critical. Everybody coaches their own way, using the style that fits them. And I do respect coaches who are able to teach a system, stay with it, recruit to it, and have consistent success.

I'll give you one example of a coach who fit that description. John Chaney was the longtime coach at Temple University, our big conference rival when I was at UMass. He was a tough, irascible man; after one of our many tensely played games, we had to be physically separated after he came at me shouting that he was going to "choke" me and "kick [my] ass." (You can view this infamous moment on YouTube.)

We ultimately became good friends, and I respected his methods. Temple played a zone defense every year—pretty much the same zone, with variations. They practiced at 5:00 A.M., played methodical basketball, and often kept the score in the fifties. They were the antithesis of how my teams usually play, but that was Chaney's comfort zone, and he didn't like to get out of it.

His teams made a bunch of Elite Eights. One year in the mid-1980s they spent a big chunk of the season as the top-ranked team in the polls. He usually had some future pros on his teams—Eddie Jones, Aaron McKie, Rick Brunson, Derrick Battie, to name a few—so the system was good enough to prepare players to have success in the NBA.

Even though I don't have a system, I have ways I like my teams to play when we have the right personnel. My preference is for a hard-nosed man-to-man defense and a "dribble-drive" offense—which to me is the perfect hybrid of showcasing individual skills and allowing us to play as a team. I adopted it from Vance Walberg, who was then a junior college coach at Fresno City College. The dribble drive is a departure from traditional basketball, which is five passes before you shoot, or four or five screens before you create a shot for a team member. In our offense, each player who catches the ball has the ability to put it on the floor and attack the basket.

There is enormous structure to the dribble drive and at the same time enormous freedom. The freedom is that anywhere I catch the ball and begin to drive to the basket, I will have a lane completely to the rim; there shouldn't be any offensive player in my way if I drive. My teammates know the instant I start going to give me that lane. If a defensive player other than the one guarding me jumps in the lane, I should have an open man. The structure is that if I want to give the ball up, I know where everyone else is going to be. I can drive and stop and lob to a teammate. I can throw it back to the perimeter, skip it to a teammate in the corner, or find one cutting to the basket.

My dribble drive is like the Princeton offense invented by the legendary Pete Carril, with its intricate cuts and back doors—but ours is the Princeton offense on steroids. There are a couple of schemes, but most of it is reading the defense. Everything is predicated on drives, and we may get to four or five drives in one possession—with other players posting, cutting, and popping out to open spots on the perimeter. As a coach I can't orchestrate it all, and I don't want to. Instead of holding ten ropes and pulling on them, I've got six ropes.

Sometimes our "offense" is no set offense at all. When we play the kind of defense I like, the offense is more of a reaction. We're getting steals, blocked shots, and rebounding missed shots and then flying up the court and playing on instinct. Throw the ball ahead and don't even look to the bench. We're just playing. As a coach I'm whistling and skipping when it goes this way. I'm happy. We've taught them and drilled them to the point that their reactions are unselfish. The structure is in the spacing and timing.

We want them to make the play they can make, the easy play—which means that each player gravitates to his strengths. When we get the ball, run it up the court and try to score quickly. If you're a three-point shooter, shoot it. If you're a driver, drive it. If you're a post-up player, post up.

There are principles embedded within what might look to fans like pure, free-flowing, fast-break basketball. For example, Michael Kidd-Gilchrist, the "warrior" on our 2011–12 squad, was a fierce defender, a great rebounder, a good passer, and an adequate shooter. But on the fast break he was the best finisher I ever coached. He would score or get fouled ninety-nine out of a hundred times. Practice is where we work on our players' weaknesses; games are where we show their strengths. We made a rule: If Michael was ahead of you in transition, you had to give him the ball; if you didn't, you were coming out of the game. So how did we play? When we were on the break, he ran like hell, because he knew he was getting the ball, and our guys got it to him.

This style of play is a way of saying to our players, *If you do this one thing—play defense—the rest is your thing.* It's a fun way to play. It maximizes athletic talent and rewards effort. And it showcases the individual strengths of our kids for the NBA scouts and executives who are watching.

One other thing I should make clear: We don't set out to play Showtime basketball. Now, anybody who thinks creativity isn't part of the game doesn't understand our sport. They've never watched Magic or Michael—or players from a generation back like Earl "The Pearl" Monroe, Tiny Archibald, and "Pistol" Pete Maravich—or the real old-timers like Bob Cousy. If we're fast and creative and fun to watch, I'm good with that.

But our focus is not to entertain. I don't care if it's not pretty.

If you forced me to define how we play, I'd say we grind and we fight. That's my system. I don't want us out there doing dipsy-doodles, no-look passes, 360-degree helicopter dunks. I tell the kids: "Try to impress *me*. Make us win. Everything else you want, it'll happen."

I coached the NBA's New Jersey Nets for two seasons and part of a third before I was told my time was up. Getting fired was awful at the time but not in retrospect. You lose a college job, it's hard. You're, like, marked for some reason. In the NBA it's a badge of honor: "You got fired three times. Good!"

One important lesson that I took from the pros and carried back into college coaching is the concept of giving ownership over to players. Basketball players are like anybody else. When things don't go well, they make excuses. They look around and cast blame. So I want to take as much as I can off my plate and put it on my players' plates. They're happy, but I'm happier, because at that point they're accountable.

I coached a total of 184 regular-season NBA games and took the club into the play-offs in my second year—no small accomplishment since the franchise had only gotten that far three times in the previous dozen years. (If I listed the names on the rosters of my Nets teams, the younger readers wouldn't know many of them.) Sam Cassell, my point guard in New Jersey, still talks about a team meeting we had like it was one of the great things he ever saw a coach do. We were talking about late-game situations, and I said, "Okay, game is on the line. Where do you want the ball? Is there something special I can run?" I went around the room. "Kendall [Gill], where do you want it? Left elbow? Good." I asked Keith Van Horn. I asked Sam. I asked Kerry Kittles. I wrote it all down.

What I'd done at that point was take every cop-out, every excuse off the table. My hope was not to be "right" and therefore able to say to a guy, "Hey, I got you the ball where you wanted it, so why didn't you make the shot?" The goal was to invest in each player's sense of himself—to acknowledge his strengths—and play to them. Ideally, guys in late-game situations would receive the ball in their favorite spots, hit the shots, and we'd all go running into the locker room high-fiving.

Even though it was the NBA and I was coaching men and not teenage boys, I tried to respect their goals and aspirations and to understand that they wanted to feel like they were growing and achieving. It was a version of Players First, though I didn't call it that at the time.

If you look back on it, some of my young players in New Jersey benefited under me by having breakout years that led to big contracts—Keith Van Horn, Kerry Kittles, Jayson Williams.

Keith Van Horn was a rookie on the 1997–98 team, and going into the last game of the regular season, he and Sam Cassell were in just about a dead statistical tie for the team leadership in points. Our play-off position wasn't going to change no matter what happened in the game.

Sam recalls a conversation we had before tip-off. "Cal said it would be good if Keith led the team in scoring, because it probably matters to him," he says. "He knew it didn't matter to me. I'd been in the league for a while, I had two rings with Houston, so it wasn't like it was going to make my career to lead the New Jersey Nets in scoring. So I looked for Keith all game long. His scoring average ended up at 19.7 points a game; mine was 19.6.

"All that season, Cal kept encouraging Keith to shoot the ball. I never heard a coach tell a rookie to keep shooting even if he was off. But Keith had a great year. At the time, he was considered on par with Tim Duncan as the best young power forward in basketball.

"If you were a veteran player like me, Cal would allow you to have input if he respected your knowledge of the game. Sometimes I'd see something on the court and make a suggestion that wasn't part of the game plan. He'd say, 'Go ahead, Sammy, but you better be right.'"

'm never going to have a player at the college level with the basketball savvy of a Sam Cassell. It's not possible. They haven't played enough games, haven't run the point in an NBA finals game 7. But I'll definitely listen to them. They're out on the floor; I'm not.

I had a situation in 2012–13 when Kyle Wiltjer, who is six foot ten but wasn't ever as physical as we wanted him to be, felt he could post up his man and score. He came into a time-out huddle and said, "Give me the ball." When a player feels like that, I never have a moment's hesitation. I'm thrilled that he's stepped up, whether it works out or not, but it usually does—because the chances of his making it if he asks for the ball, as opposed to my calling that play, are much greater. I said to the team in the huddle, "Throw Kyle the ball." They did, and he scored a couple of times before the other coach put a player in who could guard him.

In 1995, when I was coaching at UMass, we played against Kentucky, which would go on to win the national championship, and gave them their only loss of the regular season, in a late-November game at the Palace of Auburn Hills, outside Detroit. They were number one in the country, but we were up twenty points before they came back. The lead got down to six or eight, and I was going crazy. You find out about your kids at moments like that. Marcus Camby, whom I had been coaching for three years already, came over to me and said, "Coach, look at me. Just sit down. We got this."

What I love about moments like these is not so much the confidence players are exhibiting—though that's a great thing—but the fact that they are putting everything on their own shoulders. My most successful college teams take ownership at some point in the season. It's their team. They don't play for me; they play for one another. They lean on one another. They feel their own power. But they understand it has to be organized. We still play according to our principles. If a guy is a strong lefty, he runs the right side on the fast break so he can drive it back to the middle. The right-handers run the other side. We don't all of a sudden have nonshooters tossing up shots from beyond the arc.

A player who is looking for excuses doesn't want you to put the responsibility on him. It robs him of his best self-justification, what he can tell his people back home. *Coach doesn't get me. He won't let me be me.*

But my best teams want me to get out of the way. If they're playing too fast, if it's helter-skelter, all I have to do is call a time-out and calm them down. That's the deal we have. *Go after it as hard as you can. Make plays, whatever's in front of you. If it gets too crazy, I'm here to pull you back in. I've got your back.*

want our practice environment, and the whole competitive climate of our team, to be like those blast furnaces inside the steel mills where I grew up in western Pennsylvania. Hot and uncomfortable. Out of all that fire and sweat, we'll forge something strong.

DeMarcus Cousins, a high school star from Mobile, Alabama, first committed to play for Memphis, but when I took the Kentucky job, he decided to follow me to Lexington. A fun guy to be around, he went by at least two nicknames—"Boogie" and "Big Cuz"—though there could have been others that I wasn't aware of. At six foot eleven and 270 pounds, he was an unbelievable athlete who came very close to averaging a double-double in his freshman season (15 points, 9.9 rebounds), a rarity in college basketball. He was a handful for any opponent to contain and, as I learned (and his coaches in the NBA would find out), sometimes a handful to coach.

When I was recruiting DeMarcus, I knew he was not choosing a college without his mother's approval. When I asked her why she had sent him to me, she said, "Because he respected you as a coach, and I knew you weren't afraid of him."

My players have to get through fifteen conditioning drills and meet certain benchmarks before we start practice in the middle of October. The very first day, DeMarcus stopped halfway through and said, "My feet are on fire!" The whole rest of the team was watching this—the new guys who had come in with him, like John Wall and Eric Bledsoe, along with Darius Miller and DeAndre Liggins and some of the others who were already in Lexington when I took over. Everything stopped for a moment, like it does when there's a car accident and traffic comes to a standstill. First I told the other guys, "Keep going. Don't worry about him," and they picked it back up.

I turned around and DeMarcus was sitting against a wall. He had his shoes off. I walked over there and he said it again: "My feet are on fire!"

I said to him, very calmly, "DeMarcus, you didn't make that run, so you know you're going to have to make it up. And to be honest with you, I'm okay with that. I know you've got a long way to go. But you do know that you will never start for this basketball team if you can't do the conditioning and you're not in shape. You know that, right? You'll come off the bench, and if you're playing well and in shape, might play thirty minutes. But if you're not, you'll come off the bench and you'll play eight minutes. Either way, you can never start here. You do know that, right?"

He made every conditioning drill after that, every single one. It was one of those things where I could have gone crazy on him. And believe me, I do go crazy sometimes. But right then he just needed to know that, number one, respect what we're doing here. We're a team, we're in this together, and it's not going to work if one guy is sitting down with his shoes off. And number two, I wanted him to feel like I cared about him enough to encourage him to do the right thing. We were all just getting started and getting to know one another. I didn't need to humiliate him. I trusted him to know what he had to do. If I didn't believe, that I would never have recruited him.

My Kentucky teams are at their best when we just physically and mentally overwhelm teams, when we "whomp" on them, as I sometimes put it. And when we're able to do this, it's not just because I recruited a whole bunch of McDonald's All-Americans—although I know that's what some people think. It's because of what goes on inside the Joe Craft Center—on our practice floor and in our weight room.

I tell my players that we're going to play games in which it will come down to our will against some other team's will. Our opponent will have a whole bunch of talent. In the games that matter most to us, they'll have McDonald's All-Americans of their own. They'll be well-coached, confident, and physical. The chances are they average about two years older than us at every position.

"Are you going to strive?" I ask my players. "Are you going to play every single minute like you're in a dogfight? Are you going to keep mental focus when you're pushed to your physical limit? Will you vow never to give up on a teammate, that you'll keep fighting alongside your brothers for every second you're on the court?"

Will we—as individuals and as a team—build ourselves to such a level of toughness that we control games and no one controls us? That means we play at our pace, whatever we decide we want that to be. When we're running, nobody slows us down. When we slow it down, nobody speeds us up. However we want to play it, we impose that on the opponent.

These are not easy goals to achieve, and they are even more difficult because I often don't have my best players for very long.

Everything we do, every stage of our growth, has to be sped up. Their physical development in the weight room. Their mental development. Our process of team bonding—from a collection of all-star high school players into a championship college basketball team. "He teaches fast, and if you don't get it, you get left behind," is how DeMarcus Cousins puts it.

We go at it hard five or six days a week—twice a day when we can. I've got no choice. I tell my guys sometimes that it's unfair in a way. It's so condensed. In the normal process—or the process that used to exist—if you didn't get it as a freshman, you just didn't get to play as much. If it took three years, or four years, fine.

But now, maybe you're still trying to figure us out and the coaches are putting all this on you, and they're speeding you up. But we're not going to feel sorry for you. All the guys coaching with me had to fight our butts off to survive. Kenny Payne likes to say, "You need somebody to sing 'Kumbaya' to you? This ain't the staff."

I tell our kids that what we do here, it's not for everybody. But you're here for two reasons: Number one, we thought you could handle it. That's why we gave you a scholarship. Number two, you signed up for it. We warned you how hard it would be, and you made the choice to come here.

When we recruit kids and they come for a campus visit and observe a practice, I'll ask my current players a question. "How many of you knew when you came here how hard this would be? Raise your hand if you were told." And they all raise their hands. "Okay, now raise two hands if this is way harder than you thought it would be." Now everybody has two hands in the air.

CHAPTER 3

THE KENTUCKY EFFECT

I've just written about the demands we put on our players, the sacrifices we ask of them, and, to an extent, the risks they take. For some it might be too hard and it won't work out for them. Or they might not play as much as they would somewhere else, and they can't handle that.

But they encounter something else here that is beyond what I can fully explain to kids who are still in high school. They don't really feel it until they officially arrive in Big Blue Nation. I refer to it as the Kentucky Effect. Everything that happens here—on and off the court—is magnified.

When class is not in session but we're practicing, the NCAA allows us to take the players out for a meal. We usually do dinner. When we walk into a restaurant, everything stops. Some people actually rise to their feet and applaud.

It's a man's decision to play basketball at Kentucky, and not solely because of the physical demands. You're in the spotlight even when you would rather not be. If you want to smoke, you want to chase girls, you want to go to clubs, you want to do all that, this is not the place for you, because it will get noticed—and it will be splashed all over the news. At other places it might not matter as much, but if you put yourself in the middle of something like that and you play for Kentucky, the story has legs. You want it to go away, but it won't.

There are no "off" games for us, no matchups where we get anything less than our opponent's best effort. For every team we play, it's their Super Bowl. We go into an opposing gym where the attendance is usually about four thousand. For our game, it's packed to the rafters. We're looking up at sixteen thousand people, and they're totally amped.

When somebody beats us, it's a celebration. They're happy, and a lot of other people are happy too. If we hit a bump and have a down year, nobody feels sorry for us. *Kentucky lost again? Great! How many in a row is that for them? Three? Awesome! They might not even make the tournament? That's all I want for Christmas.* Really, not kidding.

If you play for Kentucky, you're a target. You're a mark. It's one of the things you have to deal with. The bright spotlight on us means that as a player you will be exposed for what you are, whatever it is. Good or bad. I can't hide you. There's no hiding at Kentucky. Your opponent wanted your scholarship. He's got something to prove. He's playing to beat you, not just Kentucky.

The verdict on you may seem to come more quickly, and that can be difficult and even a little unfair. If you don't truly have it in you, or you're not making the effort to get better—you're not grinding—it will be known sooner here than it would be somewhere else.

We try to make sure we get the kids we are supposed to and let the others go elsewhere. If you're not ready, you can't make it here—and by "ready" I don't just mean in terms of your athleticism and skill level. You have to be strong willed. You can't have a mental picture of yourself that's not accurate.

The local and national press put us under intense attention and scrutiny. I don't try to wrap the players in a cocoon. In a sense, I make the spotlight a little hotter because I will publicly talk about the state of my team and the development of individual players. I won't be harsh about it, but I'll be candid. Why? Because I want them to change.

I have players who are determined to go straight from my campus into the NBA, often after seven months with me, and I will use whatever means necessary to get my point across while I still have them. I'm not going to pile on if the press is picking on a kid, and if what they're writing is inaccurate, I'll defend him to the hilt.

But I'm not in the business of sugarcoating anything. I'm not protecting you. I *can't* protect you. Sometimes you can't even protect your own children.

Pro basketball is a man's world. If you're deficient, they won't slow things down to give you remedial instruction. They may not even say much to you. They'll just leave you on the bench, and before you know it, you're out of the league. You might get a first big contract, and you're happy as heck until you realize you're not getting a second one.

Say I've got a player who struggles on defense. The guy he's guarding goes for twenty points one night—and it's not even a hard twenty points. After the game I'm going to tell the writers exactly what happened. The other team scored because I've got one kid on my team who doesn't play defense. And I'll name him. We've got smart fans—it's not like they didn't see it themselves.

Maybe the player is a little slow, or he needs to put on weight, or he's smaller than the guys he's guarding. I say to him, "You know what, Larry Bird was slow later in his career. Marcus Camby was thin. But those guys beat you, they tripped you, they grabbed you, they punched you in the face. They figured it out. Do you want to play or not? You do? Okay, then you better figure it out too."

Coaching is like any other kind of teaching. I'm not ever going to say to a parent, "I'm coaching your son, but I'm really sorry, he is what he is. He's slow. I can't help him. I'm just going to accept it."

That's not what I would want as a father. Anybody who ever taught one of my kids, I wanted them to use every single tool they had to make my kids the best version of themselves.

There's only one thing in my program that does not get publicized. If I suspend a player, if there's something he did that sets him out, it is never described as a suspension. To me it's no one's business but ours. The public aspect of what they do is basketball. We can talk about that. But their behavior, as it relates to team rules, is for me to know about and handle. So I'll say, "He's out because he's hurt. He's got a hamstring, a groin, I don't know what it is." Or maybe, "He's sick. We're trying to find out the extent of it."

I have a placard on my desk, a piece of blue cardboard in a frame that says on top: "I commit to my team . . ." After that it says:

I will come every day ready to hold every player
  accountable for their play.
I will care about every player's growth.
I will NOT give up on this team or individual player.
I will pray for each of you in morning Mass.

The upside of the Kentucky Effect is considerable, and it far outweighs any of the burdens. When the team succeeds—and a kid thrives individually—that, too, is magnified. Playing at Kentucky confers a pedigree. Does the NBA look more favorably on my players? I think it probably does, because the guys I've had drafted at Kentucky have not just gone on to the league; they have succeeded. In the last half-dozen years, I've had Derrick Rose, an MVP; Tyreke Evans, Rookie of the Year; and John Wall, Anthony Davis, DeMarcus Cousins, and Terrence Jones, future NBA all-stars. Michael Kidd-Gilchrist, Eric Bledsoe, and Brandon Knight will get voted into all-star games if they keep progressing. Give me those guys and an NBA franchise, and I think we'd do pretty well. (Except for the abundance of point guards— we might have to trade for another big body.)

I'll also throw in Enes Kanter, an international player from Turkey who never competed in a game for us because the NCAA ruled him ineligible. NBA scouts saw enough of him on our practice floor to make him the third pick in the 2011 draft. And we prepared him enough that he played and contributed right away with the Utah Jazz, beginning as a nineteen-year-old rookie. Enes is just short of seven feet tall. He moves well and he has good hands. If he keeps grinding, I don't know what his ceiling is.

In the last five years, six of my players were named to the

NBA's all-rookie team. No other program had more than one during that span.

We have NBA scouts and team executives in our gym at every practice. If you do something good, it will be noticed. (If you're a jagoff, they'll see that too.) I really believe that most kids who play for me in Lexington go higher in the draft than if they played somewhere else—and especially, in the years we prosper as a team. Do Anthony Davis and Michael Kidd-Gilchrist go number one and number two if we don't do what we did? Do Marquis Teague or Archie Goodwin go in the first round? Do Darius, DeAndre, or Josh even get drafted at all? Was Eric Bledsoe a first-rounder if we don't go deep in the tourney in his year? I'm not sure.

If you are part of a Final Four team at the University of Kentucky, even off the bench—maybe not even in the rotation—someone in Europe will give you a contract. I can honestly say to players: "If this team does what it can do, I promise that you're going to make money playing basketball."

I've had agents tell me they are able to get better shoe deals for our NBA players. They've been on national TV just about every game. They're already known. The shoe company doesn't have to invent our players' brand—or build up their Q score—because they already have one.

For me, even five years into this job, the Kentucky Effect is ever present. It doesn't fade into the background; it gets bigger. This is the one program where you have the whole state on your shoulders. If you look at other great college basketball states, like North Carolina, California, and Michigan, the fans are split among a whole bunch of schools. Indiana may be the closest to what we have here.

In Kentucky, not to take anything away from Louisville, it is all about this program. (Except in an area around Louisville, you'll find mostly Kentucky fans. What that means is that my words carry weight. My actions carry weight. I can move people to good or bad. I can brighten their day. I can create hope for millions of people, or I can be a sour human being, coach my team, watch tape, and otherwise be absent. But that would mean cheating the position.)

It's not so much being the coach of the Kentucky Wildcats as being the coach of the team representing the Commonwealth of Kentucky. It's partly a ceremonial position. People want to touch you. You've got to get out of Lexington, because they want you in their communities. It's like you're the lieutenant governor, traveling through the state, kissing babies.

After we won the national championship, we went all around with the trophy. Joe B. Hall came to some of the events with us, along with Herky Rupp, Adolph's son. We traveled by bus. We took trains. We had four thousand or five thousand people greeting us in tiny towns, more than the number of people who lived in them. They came down from the hills. Everybody needed to put their hands on the trophy. They wanted pictures. This went on for a week.

I loved every minute of it. But at the same time, I was aware that this is not an every-year thing. The position of head basketball coach at the University of Kentucky is so big, so important to people in the state—and to Wildcat fans who live in all fifty states—that it can't be directed at just one thing. We're going to win a lot more games, and go deep in NCAA tournaments, but I don't know if I'll bring any more national-championship trophies back to Lexington. I hope I do, but you have to make it about something bigger.

This brings me back to why I'm so fortunate that this job came to me when it did, and not much sooner. To be in this position, it's good if you have already been fired somewhere, or struggled so much you almost got fired. I'd already been through that. No matter what happens, the worst thing that could happen to me, professionally, already did. I'm past it.

If you came in here and you were a thirty-two-year-old from an up-and-coming program, good luck. This is a different animal. It's coming at you in a thousand different ways. To succeed here you have to have been under the gun from the media and your fan base at some point in your career. That experience is vital. You may think you're ready, but you're probably not.

CHAPTER 4

KNOCKING ON THE DOOR

We went into the 2011–12 season in the wake of what I consider two near misses—teams that with a break here or there could have been national champions. Nobody can say that either of those rosters lacked for talent. I actually began to coach my first Kentucky team in the spring of 2009, immediately after accepting the job. The NCAA tournament was still going on—it was before April 15—so I could work my squad out, and I had them for a couple of days. But it was a far different group of guys from those I'd have the following fall. For those practices I had, like, nineteen players, no assistant coaches, and a couple of managers. Nobody could play the dribble drive and they couldn't attack the basket.

I was ready to call Memphis and say, "Will you take me back?" I remember sitting on a couch after one of these sessions with my head in my hands, and Coach Hall came up and put his arm around me and said, "It's going to be fine." And it was, because help was on the way.

Three of the guys who came in as freshmen that season—John Wall, DeMarcus Cousins, and Eric Bledsoe—wanted to be with me no matter where I coached. Their mothers trusted me to coach their sons. Daniel Orton had committed to play for Kentucky, but to the previous coach. The first trip I took was to Oklahoma to tell Daniel, "This is how we're going to do this. I want you to come, and this is how you fit in." Darius was coming back for his junior season, and Patrick Patterson decided to stay.

When we gathered that fall, I took a look out on the floor and had one of those "wow" moments. The talent level on that team was ridiculous. I had never coached a team like that.

We had John and Eric—both of them now point guards in the NBA, and both on the brink of stardom. The way we lined up was sort of old school—John and Eric were just *guards,* not always *point guard* and *shooting guard.* Both of them could handle the ball; both could drive and dish or get all the way to the hoop. It was an example of my not being wedded to a system. I'll go with what I've got.

People wondered why they would want to play together. Some of the others trying to recruit them were certainly asking them that, suggesting that one guy would take the shine off the other. But Eric at that time was maybe not fully ready for the load of running the point thirty minutes a game for a national-championship contender. And there were times when John, the more advanced one—he would become the first overall pick in that June's draft—came up against defenses focused on shutting him down.

They were able to cover for each other. That's how it's supposed to work. Eric was young but totally fearless. With his fire and his fight, he could assert himself when a defense was crawling all over John. Florida tried to do that when we played them at Gainesville, and Eric went crazy—scoring twenty-five points, a remarkable performance for a freshman playing in a hostile environment. "He stepped up big time for us," John said after the game. "Every time I drove, they weren't leaving me. They were leaving him open, and he was making shots."

But John wasn't bad either. He went for nineteen points. That's how you hope it goes when you bring in great players to play with other great players. There's a multiplier effect, and they end up better than they would have been individually. They drive one another in practice—and in games, they create space that a player won't have if he's the only big-time threat on the floor.

Eric's presence obviously didn't hurt John's draft position. And Eric ended up as the eighteenth pick in the draft when he wasn't even projected as a draft pick coming out of high school. In the NBA, even while biding his time and coming off the bench with the Los Angeles Clippers, he has distinguished himself as a future star—"an offensively potent, ever-improving defensive wunderkind," as one story described him during last year's play-offs.

Chris Paul, whom Eric was playing behind, said, "Bled is one of the best guards in the league. I've said it all season long. I'm enjoying playing with him now because there's no way he can be here next year because we probably won't have the money to pay him."

The prophecy was correct. Eric was traded to the Phoenix Suns after the 2013 season. When he signs his next contract, he may end up being paid as much as John Wall or DeMarcus Cousins.

John and Eric were killers taking the ball to the basket. De-Marcus was a beast around the basket who would always make the same suggestion during time-outs: *Just get me the ball down low.* We had Patrick Patterson and Daniel Orton, big men who would also go that spring in the first round of the draft, as well as Darius Miller, DeAndre Liggins, and Josh Harrellson.

But talent alone does not guarantee anything. Just about right out of the gate, in November in front of the usual packed house in Rupp Arena, we fell behind eighteen points against Miami of Ohio. People had to be thinking, *This guy can't coach. He's got these great players and his team is about to get run out of the gym.* We came back, but it took a buzzer beater from John Wall, with half a second left on the clock, for us to win 72–70. Their coach was Charlie Coles, a great guy and a friend of mine, who passed away in the summer of 2013. The media asked him how he felt losing such a big lead. He said, "Ask that guy over there how it felt to be down eighteen points with all those NBA players on his team."

We won a whole bunch of close games early in the season—against Stanford, North Carolina, Connecticut—any of which we could have lost. When we were 15-0, I figured we could just as well have been 9-6. But going into the tournament we had won thirty-two of our thirty-four games—including our first twenty-one in a row. And a lot of those games weren't close. Our ability to mesh caught up with our talent, and we learned to whomp on teams. In late February, Tennessee gave us our second loss of the season, at Knoxville. A couple of weeks later, in the semifi-

KNOCKING ON THE DOOR | **73**

nals of the SEC tournament, we avenged that by blowing them out by twenty-nine points. DeMarcus had a big game—nineteen points and fifteen rebounds—which would have been even bigger if he had not missed ten of his seventeen foul-shot attempts.

We had just one problem, and we knew it before we ever played a game. I remember saying to John Robic, "Who's going to hit a shot when we really need one?" We did not shoot it well from the outside, which turned out to be our undoing.

Jodie Meeks had just finished his junior season when I got the Kentucky job. In a game against Tennessee that year, he scored a school-record fifty-four points—including ten three-pointers. Jodie is a terrific player, and he would have been great with us, but I don't think he saw himself in my dribble-drive offense. It wasn't natural for him. I think he figured, *This is going to be my third coach in four years. It's time for me to put my name in the draft.* And it's worked out for him—he's made it in the league—so he did the right thing. But if he had stayed, our season might have turned out differently.

We won the first three games of the NCAA tournament—over East Tennessee State, Wake Forest, and Cornell—with an average margin of victory of twenty-five points. That put us at thirty-five wins, which at the time equaled the most-ever victories by a Kentucky team.

In the regional final game at the Carrier Dome in Syracuse, we were matched up against West Virginia. We were the top seed in the region. They were the second seed—a good squad and well coached—but they did not have even one future NBA first-rounder on their roster. Their talent did not compare to ours, but it does not always come down to that.

Of the first ten three-point shots we put up against West Virginia, we did not hit one. We didn't make any of the next ten, either. Deep into the second half, we were an astounding zero for twenty. You could drop-kick the basketball twenty times and figure one of them might go in. We did not make a three-pointer until DeAndre connected with about three minutes left in the game. We finished four for thirty-two from behind the arc.

One of West Virginia's starting guards had broken his foot a few days before the game, so a kid name Joe Mazzulla—averaging 2.2 points per game—started his first game of the year against us in that regional final. He went for 17 points.

That's sports, right? It's part of what makes it great. (Not that I felt that way at the time.)

We ended up losing, 73–66, but we had their lead down to four points with twenty-four seconds left, which is unbelievable considering how we shot the ball. If we'd hit just a couple more three-pointers—if we'd been just *bad* from behind the arc, rather than historically god-awful—we would have won the game. We would have been in the Final Four along with Michigan State, Butler, and Duke.

With the guys we had, who knows what would have happened?

I always thought my last team at UMass, in 1995–96, which lost in the national semifinals, would have been national champions if the previous year's team had won just one more game and made it into the Final Four. The experience of playing in a Final Four carries over. It's invaluable. The guys who return know exactly what has to be done to become national champions. They are less overwhelmed, less anxious.

But we had a great run that first season at Kentucky. The players coming back got the benefit of that, and it set the program on a course. I made a statement that drove some people crazy. After we had five guys drafted in the first round that spring, I said it might be the biggest moment in the history of the program. People said, *But you didn't win. How can you say that?* But the foundation was laid that projected us to another level for how many years? Every kid out there now had his mind on Kentucky. You can say what you want to say, but that's what did it. I wish we had won the national championship that first season, but we just couldn't shoot it at all against West Virginia. We knew right from the start that could be a problem, and it finally got us. But in the end, everybody did well. That, for me, is the ultimate measurement.

O f course, I don't "build" in the same way as other programs. Not enough of our best players stay. We felt pretty good getting that far in our first season in Lexington, but I had to start again the next year with a new team. Five underclassmen—including starters John Wall, Eric Bledsoe, DeMarcus Cousins, and Patrick Patterson—declared for the draft and went in the first round. The other first-rounder was Daniel Orton, a freshman who played thirteen minutes a game and averaged three points and three rebounds. Scouts had seen a little bit of him in games—and a lot of him on our practice floor.

Darius Miller, DeAndre Liggins, and Josh Harrellson returned, and they were joined in 2010–11 by freshmen Brandon Knight, Doron Lamb, and Terrence Jones. All were big-time recruits. In addition, Brandon was a straight-A student in high school, and that was important to me. I said to him, "I want you to elevate us academically. Drag your teammates with you." In the years since, our team has never been below a cumulative 3.0 grade point average. The roster, from top to bottom, was plenty good enough for our players to believe they could compete with any team in the nation. But they were not as blindingly talented as the previous group, and we did not whomp on teams in the same way or steamroller through our schedule. This team had a chip on its shoulder. That's one of the ways that one year builds into the next. All they heard was that they weren't as talented as last year's group, and they didn't like that. They got tired of it. You don't consciously play one team off against another, but your players are aware of who preceded them. They compare themselves. And they definitely don't like it when others compare them unfavorably.

We finished with a 22-8 regular-season record and a very average 10-6 record in our conference. We struggled on the road, losing at Georgia, Alabama, Ole Miss, Florida, Vanderbilt, and Arkansas. Most of those were very close at the end. We hadn't yet figured out how to close games, which is typical of young teams.

And, at times, we just looked in over our heads. At a holiday tournament in Hawaii, we lost 84–67 to Connecticut, but the game wasn't really even that close. We were down twenty-one at the half and never really in it. Brandon Knight tried to take every shot. He attempted eight three-pointers, none of which he made. I don't usually like it when parents try to coach their kids, but sometimes they say exactly the right things. On the way back to the hotel, I overheard Brandon's father say to him, "Hey, Brandon, you're not at Pine Crest anymore," a reference to his high school in Florida. "Pass the ball."

Early in February we had a stretch where we lost three out of four games—a real contrast to the team the previous season, which lost just two of its first thirty-five. But we started coming together and won the SEC tournament with a final-game 70–54 victory over Florida, which was the nation's twelfth-ranked team.

We went into the NCAA tournament with a fourth seed in the East region and just barely survived Princeton. Brandon was the kind of strong-willed point guard I love, and he proved it against Princeton. He had a horrible game and didn't score at all in the first thirty-nine minutes. But with two seconds left, he blew by his defender and floated a layup high off the backboard to give us a 59–57 win—thereby breaking the heart of every single basketball fan in America who was not a Kentucky fan. (I totally get it; if I hadn't been the coach of Kentucky, *I* would have been rooting for Princeton.)

The game-winning shot against Princeton was just the beginning of Brandon's heroics. In the next game, against West Virginia, he went bonkers, scoring thirty points. That's an unusually high point total on my teams, because our scoring is usually pretty equally distributed, but he was feeling it. Then, against heavily favored Ohio State, we were tied at sixty, with the ball. I decided not to call a time-out. Brandon had the ball on the dribble, on the right elbow, about fifteen feet from the hoop. With five seconds left, he elevated for his jump shot, let it go with a relaxed stroke, and nailed it.

For the second time in my two years at Kentucky, we were moving on to the regional finals.

I mentioned Josh Harrellson earlier, and it wouldn't be fair if I didn't come back to his story right here. Josh's willingness to change and his newfound determination paid off for him and the team. Without him we wouldn't get to the Final Four. He had been a bench player known more for his choice in shorts—he favored jean shorts, hence his nickname, "Jorts"—than his performance on the court.

But midway through the season he had a couple of breakout games, including in an upset win at Louisville. By the end of the season he was one of the best big men in the nation. His work in the weight room, his prepractice sessions with Kenny Payne, and probably his determination to prove me wrong—it all paid off. In the upset over Ohio State, he guarded Jared Sullinger, whom many regarded as the top player in the tournament, and held him in check. And Josh finished with seventeen points and ten rebounds. What had happened at the beginning of the season—his tweeting and my getting mad at him—in retrospect was something I would never have anticipated. It was a turning point. Life changed for him and for us. It's a pretty good lesson in not giving up on kids and giving them every possible chance to do the right thing.

Josh was equally important in the win over North Carolina that put us in the Final Four. In that game, Brandon led us with twenty-two points, but the scoring distribution was much more typical. We had five players in double figures, and a sixth (Doron Lamb) with eight points. It would be my third Final Four, after having previously taken teams from UMass and Memphis.

By virtue of our record and seeding, it may have seemed like a big upset for us to be among the four teams playing at Reliant Stadium in Houston. But I didn't feel that way. We had come together late, but by that point in the season (the Princeton game notwithstanding), we were really good.

In the semifinal we played Connecticut. I thought we were the two best teams left in the tournament. We shot 33 percent from the floor. Even worse, we also shot 33 percent from the foul line—four for twelve. (We hadn't been bad during the year—71 percent.) Connecticut, which would go on to defeat Butler two nights later, came away with a 56–55 victory.

If we made some plays and just hit one more shot, I thought, we'd be national champions.

CHAPTER 5

CHAMPIONS AT LAST

I don't think very much at all about plays that happened in our games during the 2011–12 season. It's not how I'm wired. If I'm thinking about a game, it's the next game. But I do think a lot about the guys, the relationships, the moments that moved us forward, the incredible examples of shared sacrifice and generosity among teammates that made us champions.

It begins with Darius Miller. He was a Kentucky kid and a former "Mr. Basketball" in the state who had led his high school team to a state championship. When I got to Kentucky, he was coming into his sophomore season and was the only guy coming back who I thought could play the dribble drive the way I wanted it. At six foot eight and about 220 pounds, he needed to change his body some and become more athletic. But he already had the ability to put the ball on the floor and physically get to the rim. He had the midrange game and the runners and pull-up jumpers you need, and he could shoot it from beyond the three-point line.

My first year he was a starter on and off. The next season, as a junior, he started just about every game and was the SEC Tournament MVP. As he came into his last season, we'd brought in a bunch of new guys. Not everybody could be a starter. I called him in and said, "Darius, I have to tell you that I want you to come off the bench. It's not going to change anything you do, but I can't start six guys.

"Here's how I see it playing out," I continued. "You're still going to be one of our top shot takers. And you're going to be one of our key guys. That ain't changing. The minutes will add up. My sixth man might play up to thirty minutes a game, so you're going to be fine. Ultimately, I think it's going to benefit you."

Keep in mind that Darius was the senior. He was a kid who had stayed in state, and he had *earned* that starting position and done nothing wrong to lose it. (By the time he was done, he would play in 152 games for Kentucky, more than anyone in the century-long history of the program.)

He didn't blink. He didn't express disappointment. He just said, "I'll do whatever you want. I'll do whatever the team needs." He practiced; he worked his butt off. There were games where he took over and led us.

People ask, "How do you get players like him to come off the bench?" Well, part of it is they may not ask, "What's in it for me?" but they wouldn't be human if they weren't thinking it. You've got to tell them what the road looks like ahead. You've got to give them that reassurance.

As their coach, I have to understand they have their own goals. Their lives are stretched out before them. This is the place where they can change their fortunes—and their families' fortunes. I can't tell them, "Just do this for us," and leave it at that.

I remind them that their personal goals and the goals we share as a team run along parallel tracks. We reach them together if everything goes as we hope.

The next thing I did was call in the six guys I considered starters. Obviously, Anthony Davis was going to start. And Marquis Teague, because he was our point guard. The other three were Michael Kidd-Gilchrist, a freshman, and Terrence Jones and Doron Lamb, both sophomores. I told them that Darius was coming off the bench, but we had six starters. And that's the way I announced it. Darius would be named Sixth Man of the Year in our conference, but in our minds he was a starter.

Darius was not the only one on that team who had to be in a giving mode even before the season began. Terrence Jones and Doron Lamb had been in the program for a season. They had played in a Final Four. But those guys were not coming back to inherit the mantle of stars or marquee performers. They had to accept three extremely assertive freshmen as teammates. They had to accept one of them, Michael Kidd-Gilchrist, as a forceful and sometimes vocal leader.

People talk about the freshmen on that team, and rightly so, but the championship doesn't happen without the returnees. We added talent to talent. The freshmen joined a group of talented players who already had an idea of what we do here and had a strong sense of team. It was a potent mix.

When I first saw Terrence as a high schooler, I thought, *Oh, my God.* A six-foot-nine left-hander, he could play underneath or shoot it from beyond the arc. His length, his speed, his physical strength, the fact that he was an unbelievable passer with the mentality of a point guard—it all jumped out at me. His habit was to drift in and out. He played and then he didn't play, which isn't that unusual among the kids I recruit. You understand it— it's hard for a player to keep pushing when he's the best guy on the floor even when he coasts—but you don't accept it.

Terrence had originally committed to play at the University of Washington, then called me after the press conference and said he had made a mistake. We had been given every indication from family and friends that he was committing to us and had been totally caught off guard when he chose Washington. So when he called back and said, "Coach, I'd rather play for you," I was surprised again, but that was all I needed to hear.

Doron was another player who, when I first saw him, I thought, *This kid is ridiculous.* But he impressed me in a totally different way. He didn't play above the rim even though he was six foot five. With Doron, you're talking about somebody who had a ton of ways to score baskets. He was a knockdown three-point shooter who also could make the little runners from six to eight feet out, and he could get all the way to the rim and make layups. He could slide over and play the point. Players with his sophisticated skill set and feel for the game are hard to find, probably even more so than the freakish athletes.

You can't have a whole team with just runners, rebounders, and defenders. You need shooters. And not only could Doron shoot it, but he could shoot it under pressure. He could make a shot when the game was on the line.

Could he have done a little more? Elevated his game? Yeah, I think so. He could have been more focused on it, could have added more intensity—and I think he'll do that in his pro career—but the reality is, he came to us so skilled that he gave us exactly what we needed.

Terrence had wanted to be a top-ten pick after his freshman season, and when he found out he wasn't, he came back. Doron wanted to go, too, but he might not have been drafted at all. They returned with a sense of unfinished business—from both an individual and a team perspective. They absolutely knew how close we had been to getting by Connecticut the previous season and what that would have meant.

The two of them, along with Darius, returned to the practice court that fall with no sense of entitlement. They were already good teammates, but it was as if they said, *Okay, now we're going to become even better teammates.* They gave the new kids exactly what they needed: the space and freedom to settle in and let their own games flourish.

When Anthony Davis first arrived on campus, the summer before his freshman year, our college president, Dr. Lee Todd, Jr., looked at him and said, "Wow! I love this kid. He's going to be here a few years. Somebody this skinny can't go to the NBA right away."

I didn't try to correct him; I just smiled.

Anthony was the opposite of the kids you read about who are identified as future superstars while still in grade school and followed all the way up by recruiting services and the media. When he started ninth grade he was six feet tall. He was a guard.

He grew an inch or two before his sophomore year, then sprouted to six foot seven before his junior season—and six foot ten as a senior.

Obviously, at that point you're talking about an entirely different player, one who has been working on his perimeter skills since he first picked up a basketball but is now just an inch under seven feet tall—and still the fastest kid on the floor. Kenny Payne heard about Anthony and one day said to me, "There's a kid in Chicago everybody is talking about. He just grew six inches. We need to go see him."

The first time I watched him was at a tournament in Indiana. I don't like to compare one player to another, but my first thought was, *This is another Marcus Camby.* His build, his gait, his desire to challenge every shot all reminded me of Marcus. Whenever I have a kid like that, my teams do well.

Anthony's high school team was one of the worst I'd ever seen. Perspectives Charter School, which he had attended since the sixth grade, specialized in first-rate math and science instruction, not basketball. That's why he was enrolled there. It's why he was a good student during his time at Kentucky. But they won six games one year, seven the next year. And that was *with* Anthony Davis.

I met with his family, his grandparents. He was a just a great kid. Just about the first thing he said to me was, "You tell me what you want me to do. I just want to win. That's all I care about."

Anthony and Michael Kidd-Gilchrist knew each other from the AAU circuit, and they wanted to play together. But Michael's talent had been spotted at a much younger age. He announced publicly, in eighth grade, "I want to play for Coach Cal at Memphis," which he amended to Kentucky when I changed jobs.

I knew what he was from the first moment I saw him—an absolute warrior. "One thing I want you to do when you get here is drag this team forward with your work ethic, your will to win, your strength of mind," I said to him before our season. "That is absolutely a skill you have."

When Michael started classes that year, he was still seventeen years old. But certain players just naturally elevate an entire group, which is what Michael did—by both word and deed. He had some flaws in his game. He was a spotty shooter, but he just willed balls into the basket and sometimes you didn't know how—they just went in. When they didn't go in, he was following them up. I don't know how many put-backs of his own shots he had that season, but it was a lot.

He was one of the best I've ever had at letting me define his game. Michael knew his shooting was suspect, so he came to practice early every day, and we gave him areas where we knew he could make shots and said, "Here are your best spots. Left elbow. Right elbow. One-dribble pull-ups. Let's work on those until you're knockdown from there."

It was another example of building on strengths. You don't have to be good at everything in our game. There are NBA players who have made tens of millions of dollars by perfecting just one offensive move—and maybe a variation or two on that move. If it's unstoppable, you don't *need* anything else. (Michael was by no means unstoppable, except on the fast break, but he very quickly made himself into a formidable offensive force in the college game.)

I wrote about how players have to learn to love the grind, but Michael already loved it before he got here. Our kids that year followed his lead. He had heard about a tradition that Michael Jordan began in Chicago, which he called the Breakfast Club. His Bulls teammates would come to Jordan's house in the morning, his chef would cook them breakfast, and they would lift weights. So Michael Kidd-Gilchrist started the same thing at Kentucky. In the mornings before class, he was at the gym—lifting, stretching, practicing his ball handling, shooting—and he'd usually drag five or six guys with him.

When players combine elite athleticism and great determination, you don't worry too much about position. You just know you have something good, and their skill sets will improve. On our 2011–12 team, Marquis Teague and Doron Lamb played, for the most part, traditional positions—point guard and shooting guard. Anthony, I guess, was our center, to the extent we had one—he was our tallest guy—but he could rebound the ball, bust out with it on the dribble, and lead a fast break. He could shoot it from three-point range, though he rarely took those shots.

Terrence, as I've mentioned, could play all over the court. When Darius came in the game, he could play on the wing and also bang some inside. So we were really free flowing, flexible, and hard to defend—right down to Kyle Wiltjer, our other freshman, who mostly spotted up on the perimeter and shot three-pointers but, at six foot ten, was also developing an ability to post up smaller defenders.

Michael had played around the basket in high school, and with his strength I could have played him at power forward. You can easily win in college basketball with an undersized "4," but I wasn't going to do that to him. In the NBA, at six foot seven, he was going to be a small forward, so those are the skills we gave him and the spot where we showcased him.

Our whole team that year, not just Michael, was ultracompetitive. I knew that our practices would be vicious—guys just going after one another—and that is exactly what happened. Teammates sometimes got nose to nose, which happens when you practice hard. You're banging on the same guy day after day; tempers flare.

I don't want them having fights in practice. That's just stupid. But I want the kind of intensity where they're right on the edge of that. We didn't have one bad practice all year, which is an amazing thing for a coach to be able to say.

We started out the year with games at Rupp Arena against Transylvania and Morehouse in exhibitions and the season opener against Marist, and feasted—averaging 110 points in three victories. The Morehouse score was 125–40, even though I cleared the bench early and none of my starters played more than twenty-four minutes.

Even with those big margins of victory, you learn something about your kids. In this case, I saw their hunger—they really liked dominating—and also their generosity and sense of responsibility to the deep subs and walk-ons on the bench. Those guys have to put up the best fight they can in practice, even when they're physically overmatched. They're not just window dressing. They've got a job that matters to us.

We had Jarrod Polson, Sam Malone, Twany Beckham, and Brian Long on that team, along with Eloy Vargas, who often got some meaningful minutes spelling the big men and later went on to play for the Dominican Republic national team and professionally in Hungary. The players in the regular rotation really liked running up big leads so those guys could get in the game. Then they sat on the bench and cheered their brains out for them.

Our level of competition increased exponentially in our second game. We played Kansas at Madison Square Garden in New York. The media called it an "early-season test" for our highly touted freshmen. Stories written before and after also made sure to point out that Kansas and its coach, Bill Self, were the opponents when my Memphis team had the bottom fall out and lost the big lead in the 2008 NCAA title game. I always enjoyed reading about that. The game was also a preview of sorts—but we had no way of knowing that at the time.

It being so early in the season, neither of the teams were nearly as good as they would become. The first half was ugly, like a heavyweight fight with two boxers leaning against each other and throwing weak punches. It ended 28–28. We went on an 11–0 run early in the second half that began with a thunderous dunk from Terrence—he made sure to mug for a TV camera after throwing it down—and featured a three-pointer and pretty floater from Marquis.

Doron, who scored seventeen points, told reporters afterward, "I think we made a good statement today," but I didn't see it that way. We had five guys in double figures, which I really like. (My goal in any season is to have six players average double figures.) We showed a strong will to win, which never wavered with this group. But we were sloppy and impatient. We cut off plays, with too many guys trying to make moves on their own. We turned the ball over nineteen times, which is way too many.

I told our players afterward that they weren't in Orlando anymore, which is where they play the big AAU tournaments. We didn't have another game the next morning, then the next afternoon. We weren't going to Disneyworld before we went home. This was Kentucky basketball. Our games are on national TV. We only play them a couple of times a week, and every moment of every game counts. I said we were showing that we had good players, but we weren't yet a good team. I wasn't being dramatic—I was being honest. We had a long way to go.

Two weeks later we played St. John's in Lexington. If you just looked at the box score, you'd say: *All good. They're doing what they're supposed to do. Right on schedule.* We coasted to an 81–59 victory, pushed our record to 7-0, and never really seemed threatened. Anthony had fifteen points, fifteen rebounds, and eight blocked shots. If I'd let him play longer, he would have had a triple-double. Everyone was happy in Big Blue Nation.

We had consecutive games coming up against North Carolina and Indiana. The press wanted to know how I was feeling. I told them that if we played like we just had, I'd be a very sad coach after those games.

What I said to my team behind closed doors was much stronger than that. I thought we had stunk. We had no offensive flow. We were winning with our physicality and talent, but at a certain point you have to execute because you'll come up against other teams with great players—and those teams *will* execute. Just going at it really hard won't get it done. Players have to listen closely and play the way we want them to.

When you start playing good teams, and we call one thing in a time-out and you go out and do something different, you lose. That's how it works. So at a certain point, you've got to start playing the right way. Talent alone doesn't prevail.

I'm not a coach who breaks the schedule down in stages—preseason, nonconference, conference, conference tourney, NCAAs—and sets goals or benchmarks for where I want us to be at each point. It's more organic. What I want is to be able to visually see that we're getting better. Are we correcting our errors? Is what we're doing in practice carrying over into games? Are we playing the right way?

And we weren't doing any of those things. We were purely results oriented. *We won again? Great, let's just move on.* My job is to get in the way of that thinking. Sorry, but we're not just moving on. We're fixing it.

Bob Rotella, a close friend and sports psychologist I have consulted for a couple of decades now, happened to be with us for the St. John's game, and he was in the locker room afterward. "Cal chewed them out," is how he remembers it. "They might have been a little surprised, because they felt good about themselves, but he told them what he was seeing wasn't nearly good enough. They were young. They hadn't been through it before. He was saying, 'Look guys, I know this stuff. I've done it before and you haven't. It's not about winning and losing. The results take care of themselves. I'm seeing mistakes that I won't tolerate.'

"He didn't like their effort the last seven minutes and their at-tention to detail over the whole game. It may have been the sin-gle most important moment of the year. This is where he made it clear how high the bar was. This team had incredible desire. They had the same goals he did. But he was saying that if you want to reach them, you have to believe me when I say we're not as good right now as you think we are."

I agree with Rotella that I got their attention that night, but we didn't solve everything all at once. It doesn't work that way. Two days after St. John's, we slipped past North Carolina, 73–72. That kept a couple of things going.

Thirty-nine-game Rupp Arena winning streak preserved: *check*.

Number one national ranking maintained: *check*.

But we were vulnerable. We would have lost against North Carolina except that Anthony saved us. North Carolina's John Henson had a clear shot for a jumper with a couple seconds left, but Anthony came from the other side of the lane and just about jumped out of the building to get up and swat the ball away.

As a coach you love heroics like that. It's not that different from being a fan. You say, *Wow! That was amazing!* It was excit-ing. You ask kids to make plays when it counts, and that's a play. It's stepping up.

But there's a rational side of you that doesn't trust it. If you need someone to be Superman at the end to win games, you're going to lose games.

Our next game, against Indiana in Bloomington, was what finally caused us to grow up. We went into the locker room at half-time trailing by just one point. Four minutes into the second half—after three turnovers, a missed dunk, and nothing but careless, brain-dead play on both offense and defense—we were down ten points. We clawed back, and Indiana had to hit a last-second three-pointer to get the victory, but our players knew that what beat us was the way we had played for the first thirty-nine minutes.

I was livid going back down the hallway to the locker room—livid!—not because the team had lost but because the players hadn't listened: right down to the last time-out, when we told them to foul because we had two fouls to give before Indiana was in the bonus and free throws, and they didn't get that done. The whole game we hadn't been on the same page. Everybody was worrying about themselves.

If you do everything right and the other team just makes a play and beats you, you can live with that. But that wasn't what happened. Michael Kidd-Gilchrist cried after the game. A bunch of the kids came up to me the next day and said, "This will never happen again."

I wrote earlier that it was after the Indiana game, in which he had helped key our comeback, that Marquis Teague "surrendered"—the word we use to mean that a player accepts our coaching. A player who surrenders finally acknowledges that the way he's playing—even if it's how he has *always* played—isn't working anymore. He can no longer count on just physically dominating the player he's going up against, because he's moved up to a new level of competition. His teammates are better, and he needs to include them.

It reminds me of an experience I had at a fantasy camp I run in the summers for adult recreational players. Most of them are Kentucky fans, successful in their chosen fields, decent athletes. In one of my camps I was coaching a player named Ric Elias, the cofounder and CEO of Red Ventures, a big marketing firm in Charlotte, North Carolina. Fascinating guy. Among other things, he was on the US Airways flight in 2009 that Chesley "Sully" Sullenberger had to ditch in the Hudson River. He was standing on the wing when he got rescued.

I was coaching Ric's team and had to tell him he was playing too fast, forcing plays rather than letting them develop. "Fast feet, slow mind," I said to him.

He came up to me later that day and said, "You are so right. It's funny because that is how I run our company. It's how I operate. I'm sprinting through the day, but at the same time I'm evaluating at a different speed. It's like having two tracks running at the same time. The second one is the internal dialogue that I'm constantly running. People ask me how I'm doing so many different things at the same time, but it doesn't feel that way to me. In my own mind I don't feel rushed."

It made me think of Marquis and all the other point guards I've coached. That's exactly how I want them to play. They are all ridiculously explosive athletes with the physical makeup of NFL cornerbacks or wide receivers. At times, I don't want to slow them down. I need them to push the action, blow past defenders if they can.

They have to be the storm—*and* the calm within the storm. Wow. How do you express that to a young kid?

Sometimes I say it's unfair what we do at Kentucky, how we aim so high and load so much on our players in such a short period of time. It's especially unfair to my point guards because no other position compares to its degree of difficulty. But one thing I don't get is when I hear people say that it's "hard" to play point guard for me. Hard compared to what? Hard compared to if I didn't coach them as intensely? Hard compared to playing for somebody else and not getting picked in the first round of the NBA draft?

My ego isn't wrapped up in turning out John Calipari-branded point guards, and I don't consider my expectations to be too high. I think of the point guards we've sent off to the NBA. I guess I could have made it easier on them, but what point would that have served? I guarantee you they're not looking back and thinking they'd be better off if I'd cut them a break.

Marquis helped get us into a hole in that Indiana game with a bunch of bad shots and by not passing when he should have. The irony is that he also helped dig us out. He's an Indiana kid with a huge competitive heart, and the game may have had some extra meaning for him. In the second half he made five or six incredible plays and just about willed us to victory.

I don't want it to seem like his struggle to learn the position—a normal learning curve for a young point guard—was the only issue we had. It was just magnified because of the importance of his position. When he came to me and said he knew he needed to change, it gave us a chance to be a more fluid, more efficient team.

We had a team meeting after that and I reaffirmed what I had told Marquis in front of everyone. I said, "I want you all to know I am with Marquis Teague. He knows he's got to get better and he's got to change some things. He's going to be fine, and we're going to be fine."

It was an absolutely key moment in our season, and everybody on the team knew it. They kind of looked at each other and said, "Okay, it's on now. It's on."

And it was. We won a bruising game against archrival Louisville at noon on New Year's Eve. Jay-Z was sitting courtside, along with the usual couple of dozen NBA scouts and executives.

We won because Michael Kidd-Gilchrist just put us on his shoulders. He finished with twenty-four points and nineteen rebounds. I played him thirty-nine minutes, which I never do, but he was that good—and his conditioning allowed me to keep him on the court.

It was a game in which both teams were just crashing into each other, and guys were flying into the stands going after loose balls. When one of the writers asked Michael in the interview room about the physical play, he smiled and said, "I'm built for this."

We blew through our conference schedule. After struggling on the road the previous season, winning just two conference games away from Lexington, we won in Knoxville, Athens, Baton Rouge, Columbia, and Nashville.

Our final conference game was in Gainesville against a very good Florida team. We were undefeated in the SEC. We had won twenty-one straight games and had long ago clinched a number one seed in the conference tourney and probably the NCAA tournament as well. One more win would give us thirty victories—a regular-season record for a Kentucky team. I told the team that nothing would change if we lose. Just go out and have fun and play for pride, I said. Those were the stakes I set.

We were, by then, a brutally efficient team. I wrote earlier that I want to visually see us progress as a team, but like any coach, I keep a close watch on statistics, which tell their own story. Pick any stat you want from that year. Over the course of our forty games, we outscored our opponents by a total of 672 points—an average victory margin of just about seventeen points a game. We shot 48 percent to our opponents' 37 percent. We made more foul shots than the other teams attempted. We had almost three times as many blocked shots. We would have achieved my goal of six guys scoring in double figures, except that Darius Miller came up just short, finishing at 9.9 points a game.

There are more granular stats that our coaching staff looks at. One of the main ones is points per possession. How many points do you get on each trip down the floor? Ideally, you want a point per possession, and if you achieve that, you're doing pretty well. On defense you're trying to hold them under a point—0.75 or 0.8 per possession. It's just a numbers game. Do both of those things, and you'll win comfortably.

Underneath the numbers is the story of how you played. Did you fight for the offensive rebounds that lead to second shot attempts? How many possessions did you waste because of turnovers? What was the quality of your shots? What shots did you force the other team into taking? (We chart offensive rebound *attempts*, meaning effort.)

On offense it starts with driving the ball to the basket, which produces high-percentage layups—or even better, dunks. Or you get fouled, which, if you shoot a decent percentage from the line, results in about a point and a half per possession.

The second option is a quality three-point attempt. Even if you hit just 35 percent of your three-pointers, it's better than shooting 50 percent from inside the line. The worst shot is a midrange jumper. A lot of basketball fans say: *Nobody can make a twelve-foot jump shot anymore!* It offends them, and I understand why. A professional basketball player or big-time college player ought to be able to knock that shot down, especially if he's unguarded. But the numbers tell you why they don't practice those shots enough. Even in the NBA, where the three-point arc is farther out, most of the best teams are near the top in three-point shots attempted and percentage of three-pointers made.

On defense our priorities are the converse of what they are when we have the ball. Guard the basket. Guard the three-point line. Force turnovers. Rebound every missed shot. We'll take our chances getting beaten by teams hitting midrange shots. It's usually not going to happen. Even when they make them, it's just two points. And there's no reason for us to foul.

The other thing that matters is matchups. Against Florida in Gainesville, with our undefeated conference record at stake, we got off to a comfortable lead, but the Gators kept chipping away at it. We were playing well but not great and went into the locker room at halftime with an eight-point lead.

They had a guy guarding Terrence who I knew couldn't play

him. I said to him simply, "Terrence, you're one of the top five players in the country. Play that way."

I'd say that kind of stuff to Terrence, to a lot of our guys. *You've made strides? Okay, you're happy. I'm happy. Now take it up a notch. That's what I'd do if I were you. Get your body better. Make your shooting better. Make it all better. Because it's in you. I know that because I'm standing here looking at you. You're pretty good, but you've only scratched the surface.*

Terrence scored fourteen points in the second half. We won, 74–59, and became just the third team since Alabama in 1956 to go undefeated in conference play. The other two were the 1996 and 2003 Kentucky teams.

I t's never easy to defeat a team for a third time, which is what you have to do in a conference tournament after you've ripped through the regular season undefeated. We began the SEC tourney by beating LSU, 60–51, then were matched up against Florida again, less than a week after beating them in Gainesville. We came away with a grind-it-out 74–71 victory.

We weren't whomping on teams, that's for sure. I could identify a lot of reasons for that—playing for no stakes; a little fatigue; a natural emotional lull before the NCAA tournament; some nervousness about what was ahead.

On the day of the SEC championship game against Vanderbilt, Michael Kidd-Gilchrist came up to me in the locker room thirty minutes before our game and said, "Coach, I want you to start Darius today. I'm not feeling right."

I took a step back and tried to see what the heck Michael was talking about. He wasn't sniffling like he had a cold. His eyes looked fine. Nobody on our training staff had mentioned anything to me. He looked great. He always looked great.

He said to me again, "Coach, I just don't want to start," and I said to him, "Michael, tell me what you're talking about."

"Well, Darius is playing awful, and you're all over him," he explained. "So I want you to let him start in my place. I think that will help him, and we need him in the NCAA tournament. It's up to you, Coach, but that's my feeling."

Michael was right about Darius being in a funk. It happens, and sometimes as a coach you have no idea why. Darius was just floating around out there. The name and number on his uniform were the same, but it was like somebody else was inside of it. A poltergeist. An imposter. I don't know who was in that uniform, but it wasn't the kid I'd known for the last three years. The Darius of the last couple of games wasn't a good player and he wasn't having any fun.

Over the first two games of the tournament he attempted only five shots. He didn't make any of them. He grabbed three rebounds and turned the ball over four times. Michael was also right when he said we needed Darius—the *real* Darius—to have any shot at winning a national title. We weren't a superdeep team. There was a big drop-off between Darius, who was named Sixth Man of the Year in the SEC, and our three-point-shooting specialist, Kyle Wiltjer, and the other guys on the bench.

In the locker room before the game, I told the team about my conversation with Michael. They were in their uniforms, waiting for me and the coaching staff to review our scouting report, tell them their defensive assignments, and go over details like what out-of-bounds plays we would run and how we'd set up if they pressed us. "There's something I need to tell you," I said. "Michael came to me and says he wants Darius to start." I stopped and pointed at Darius, just to make it clear. "He wants you to play.

"Now, that's a hell of a thing," I continued. "Normally, I'd say, 'You let me coach this team.' But I'm going to grant his wish. You guys like each other. You look after each other. You share the ball. You're unbelievable defensively. It's a big thing to give up your starting spot in a game like this on national TV, but I think we have other guys in this room who would do the same. It shows who we are. That love for each other is what sets us apart."

The game was bad. We were up 62–57 with five minutes left, then didn't do one good thing the rest of the way and lost, 71–64. Michael played very little, because once I put him in the game, he immediately got into foul trouble. Darius took seventeen shots—more than I'd wanted him to take—and made seven of them, but it didn't matter. What I liked is that he was *alive* again.

We lost our twenty-four-game winning streak and did not emerge as champions of the conference tourney, which I care *zilch* about. Overall, the result mattered very little, and it gave me a chance to get the players' attention. We played soft, we played a little arrogant, we had some guys who looked like they didn't want to take shots at the end. I'm never going to get on a kid for missing shots, but not taking a shot when it's your shot, a place on the court within your range, that's an issue.

Don't take anything away from Vandy, I told my team after the loss. They played a heck of a game. But they beat us because we didn't play the right way. "Look, we missed every single shot down the stretch. At the end we had guys not wanting to shoot it. Don't stay in the game if you feel that way. We're not worried about losing. We're playing to win.

"We were good today at saying 'my fault.' How many of them did we have today? We can't have any more 'my faults.' Now we have to be a machine. You go into this thing and it has to be like clockwork. You go back to the room, you watch the tape, you get rest and get ready for what's next.

"We've got three weekends. Don't worry about six straight games. We've got to win two next weekend. Two the next weekend. And two the weekend after that. That's how it goes. That's all we need. Now, my question is, are you going to listen to me?"

I'm not a coach who thinks that if you don't reach the ultimate goal, all is lost. You can't be happy that way. A lot of the time it's not going to work out for you. There are no UCLAs anymore that win year after year after year. I wanted to remind them to be proud of what they had already accomplished, even while pressing ahead to what we all wanted.

"Guys," I said, "you had a hell of a run. Now the real stuff starts."

Thinking about how you would try to beat your own team goes with the job of being a coach. You put yourself into the mind of another coach as he looks at film of your games. Where are we vulnerable? What defenses have we struggled against? At what speed don't we like to play?

To be honest, we didn't have glaring weaknesses. Going into the NCAA tournament, we had lost only two games. In one of them it took a buzzer-beating three-pointer to kill us, even though we had played terribly. The second one was the Vanderbilt loss, which wouldn't have happened if the game had meant more.

But I know how I would have played against my team: on offense as slowly as possible, letting the shot clock run down in every possession; and on defense in a zone, which also can have the effect of slowing a game down. Basically, I would have tried to shorten the game, make it fewer possessions, and hope for the best.

Teams had tried to play slow against us before, and it hadn't bothered us that much. But what was the alternative? With the speed and size we had all over the court, I wouldn't get in a track meet against us. The way we rebounded the ball, kicked it out, all got on the fast break, you ran the risk of our just blowing by you and putting up a whole bunch of points before you even knew what hit you.

We opened up in round 1 against Western Kentucky in Louisville. They had some fans there. They were comfortable trying to play deliberately. It wasn't the easiest matchup I could have imagined, but we handled it, and in a way I really liked. The two upperclassmen in our starting lineup took all the pressure off Marquis, Michael, and Anthony, our heralded freshman class. It was like they said, *Okay, young fellas, we got this one.*

Everyone wanted to know how those kids would respond to the glare of the NCAA tournament, but the older guys never gave them a chance to get the jitters. Terrence scored twenty-two points and added ten rebounds. Doron had sixteen points. They shot a combined sixteen for twenty-five. They were just really calm and really good.

Next we had Iowa State, followed by a rematch against Indiana. The ways those games developed were, in their own ways, testaments to our players' spirit, love for one another, and growth over the course of the season.

Iowa State basically said, *Let's blanket everybody else and let Marquis Teague try to beat us. He's a little shaky. If we give him space, he'll get too crazy and we'll take advantage of that.* Marquis put twenty-four points on them. Shot ten for fourteen. He still shared the ball and ended up with seven assists against just two turnovers.

There was no Knute Rockne speech before the Indiana game. There was nothing. Just a game plan. Here's who we're going to trap. Here's how we're going to guard Zeller, their big kid. Here's what we'll do if they press us.

I didn't *have* to say anything because that loss back in December had infuriated our guys. It gnawed at them and drove our team through the rest of the season. Even if they had wanted to put it behind them, they couldn't, because ESPN kept replaying the three-pointer that beat us, over and over again, so our kids couldn't get away from it.

There was the Indiana guard penetrating. Kicking it back to Christian Watford. Darius flew at him but couldn't get there in time. He actually crashed into Marquis after he left his feet and ended up on the floor. The shot went through the net with one second on the clock. Before Darius could get up, he was trampled by Indiana's fans rushing the court. Some of the Indiana players were up on the scorer's table, pumping their fists.

Indiana won an ESPY for that play. That's how it is—you beat us, you win an award they hand out on prime-time TV.

When we finished the regular season with just one loss—that

loss—Terrence Jones joked about getting rid of his electronics so he wouldn't have to see it anymore. "I almost sold my iPhone, my iPad," he said. "I turn the TV off. I don't watch it. I don't see it. I hear my name, I hear 'Jones,' and I change the channel."

I actually didn't mind that ESPN kept running the sequence, especially when it included Indiana's jubilant fans and players. It was a great service to us. Every time my team watched, it inspired them.

In our rematch in the regional semifinals of the tournament, Indiana tried to outrun us, get easy baskets, fly up and down and see if they could get us tired. It was one of the best games you'll ever see—just beautifully played basketball by two teams really going at each other. They played great, but they weren't beating us, not that day. Wouldn't allow it. We won, 102–90.

One other thing: Darius Miller had scored nineteen points in the previous game against Iowa State. In the Indiana game, he scored nineteen again, on six-for-eight shooting and a perfect five for five from the line.

Michael Kidd-Gilchrist, who scored twenty-four against the Hoosiers, with ten rebounds, had been right: We needed Darius, and his sacrifice helped put him back on track. What Michael did was a perfect example of how I want my players to take ownership of the team. He was invested in the whole, not just himself. He cared enough for a teammate to take a step back, a temporary one, so another kid could step forward.

I don't think anyone on that team will ever forget that. My hope is that they'll use it in their own lives—on their professional teams, in their families, in their communities. I talked in the media at the time about what Michael had done, so people closely following Kentucky basketball were aware of it, and maybe some of them, too, have benefited from his example.

W e needed to get by one last team, Baylor, to return to the Final Four. They were long and athletic like us, with a six-foot-eleven kid in Perry Jones who came into college considered a surefire lottery pick. But they weren't efficient, and under pressure could be forced into turnovers. Our margin of victory, 82–70, wasn't really indicative of how the game went. We went on a 16–0 run and were up twenty-two points before the end of the first half—and still ahead by eighteen with about three minutes left in the game. Baylor scored some late baskets after the game was out of reach.

Michael's ability to guard multiple positions, and the pride he put in his defense, allowed me tremendous flexibility. I put him on Baylor's little point guard, Pierre Jackson, and Michael just blanketed him and never let Baylor get into its offense. Terrence had a tremendous all-around game with twelve points, nine rebounds, and six assists.

"This team is better than I thought," Scott Drew, Baylor's coach, said afterward. Two years earlier his Baylor had lost in a regional final to Duke, the eventual national champions. "Duke was a good team," he said, "but Kentucky is better."

It was an interesting comment for Scott to make, because that Duke squad was loaded with upperclassmen, with three seniors and two juniors who started in the national title game. Part of the tension in college basketball every year is the contest between youth and experience. Which one wins out? Say what you want about the syndrome of "one and done," but it does make for a compelling story line.

I've been quoted as saying, "If I'm forced to choose between talent and experience, I'm taking talent every time." You can *gain* experience and you can add skills, but what's sometimes called God-given talent is just that. Coaches call it "upside"— what's in a player that we can bring out. I'm certainly not complaining about having to coach really young teams—it's a choice I make—but it does present its own unique challenges.

People talk sometimes about teams being at a size disadvantage, but less often about an age disparity. We play games every year where at every position the other team is two or three years older than us. If you think that doesn't matter, you don't know much about basketball. And you've certainly never, as a kid, gone up against a team of older guys at a playground—the stereotypical Y players—whom you think you can run off the court until they frustrate you with back doors, well-placed elbows, baby hooks, up-and-unders, pulling on your jersey, and a whole bunch of other tricks you can't deal with.

Youth very rarely wins out at any level of basketball, including the NBA. Think of the long run of excellence by the San Antonio Spurs, even as their core of key players hit their midthirties. Think of the Boston Celtics, who won the title in 2008 with a trio of Kevin Garnett, Paul Pierce, and Ray Allen, all of them well past thirty. Think of why the Brooklyn Nets traded last summer for Garnett and Pierce, making a bet on guys who were now thirty-six years old. Think of their old running mate, Ray Allen, who at thirty-eight years old hit the last-ditch three-pointer in game 6 of the NBA finals that saved the Miami Heat.

Those types of guys aren't flying around dunking the ball anymore. They get traded for because the general manager thinks they can still win. The Oklahoma Thunder, with Kevin Durant and Russell Westbrook, have been the best *young* team in the NBA for a couple of seasons. But they're still waiting for a championship, and might be for a while. We'll see.

My job is to give our players a lot of basketball knowledge in a short amount of time. They need my crash course in order to win at Kentucky. And they need it because a lot of them—eight months after they start with me—will enter into a league of grown men.

One thing I have to guard against is the tendency of my kids to look too far down the road—and also to take certain things for granted rather than pausing for reflection. I have to remind them that here is where we are. Right now. Focus on what we're doing in the moment. And don't be afraid to stop to honor the milestones you've already achieved.

What's that expression? You don't know where you're going until you know where you've been? I believe in that. I also believe that if you don't slow down and take stock sometimes, you're never going to feel good about yourself.

After we beat Baylor a couple of my older guys—sophomores—said, in effect, that it was not that big a deal. They had been to the Final Four the previous season, and they expected to be back to take care of their unfinished business. I didn't mind that. I certainly didn't want them thinking that the Final Four was an endpoint. But just as at the end of the regular season, I told everyone to hit the pause button and think about the road we'd just traveled. Celebrate it. Revel in it.

"What I want you to do is relax and enjoy what you just did," I said. "Guys, we just put this team together six months ago, and you're going to a Final Four. You won more games than any Kentucky team in history—thirty-six games is the most wins ever for a program that is a hundred years old and has won all these national titles. You've won more. How about that? What you have done, people are stunned.

"John Thompson [the former Georgetown coach] asked me, 'How do you get them to play together?' It starts with the recruiting. You're not going to take thirty shots a game here. You're going to share for each other. You all shared and every one of you has benefited. Every one of you. Enjoy what you just did."

Only at that point did I turn the focus to New Orleans, the site of the Final Four. We were going to play Louisville, which the day before had beaten Florida to win the West Regional. The hype would be out of control. I already knew that. Big Blue Nation versus its in-state rival. Kentucky versus its former coach. Calipari versus Pitino.

Louisville's season had been bumpy. After we beat them on New Year's Eve, they lost seven more times, including the last two games of their regular season. One of their losses was a 90–59 blowout at Providence. Nobody was really looking at them as one of the teams likely to show up in New Orleans, which is not a bad situation to be in for a team with Final Four–level talent.

Louisville won four straight at Madison Square Garden to capture the Big East tournament, then another four to reach

New Orleans. They were on cloud nine. Nothing to lose. Playing with house money. Even before we beat Baylor they were talking about us, telling the press, "We want Kentucky."

I told our team, "Don't even mention Louisville. Worry about us. They like to play fast. Good. We like to play fast. We're exactly where we want to be."

"We have more business to take care of," I said in the locker room after we beat Baylor. "But we're not playing a tournament. We're going down there to play a game. We're playing a basketball game. Okay? That's all we're doing."

I sleep fine before games. The last time I can remember that I didn't was many years ago, and it's interesting because it was a game that was built up too big and that I probably made too much about myself. I was at UMass. We were already good and had been to numerous NCAA tournaments, but to some people we were still upstarts.

Boston College never wanted to play us. They had no interest in an in-state rivalry and didn't want to give us credibility. I got that. They played in the vaunted Big East, and we were the mid-major from the Atlantic 10. They didn't want us infringing on their territory.

But then somebody came up with the idea of a "Governor's Cup" game to be played in the new Boston Garden. It would be the first college game in that building, and they were going to sell tickets for seventy-five, a hundred bucks, somewhere in that range. Which I thought was crazy. They weren't getting that for

NBA games. But guess what? The tickets sold out in, like, forty-five minutes.

So then all anybody could talk about was this game. For two weeks before it happened, there were stories about it on the sports page every day. It was larger than life. It was the Super Bowl. It was the Indianapolis 500.

The night before, we were in the Colonnade Hotel in Boston. We were going to play the following afternoon. I woke up and thought it was about 6:00 A.M. I had a treadmill in my room and started running on it. Halfway into my workout, I looked at the clock and it was 2:00 A.M. If I slept any more that night, it was no more than a half hour.

I remember the bad night more than the game. Boston College was good and had a future NBA player in Bill Curley and another kid, Danya Abrams, who went on to a long pro career in Europe. We fell behind in the first half because we were jittery—probably my team reading my mood—then settled down because of our guards and came away with a win.

Looking back on it, I didn't want this program I had built up at UMass to be perceived as taking a step back. And I'm sure I didn't want to personally be seen as having been knocked down a peg. One of the great luxuries of having established myself—and of being the coach at Kentucky—is that I no longer have those kinds of concerns.

But as we prepared to play Louisville, that didn't stop people from trying to make it about me. I supposedly needed a championship notch to validate my career. Rick Pitino and Bill Self, the Kansas coach, already had NCAA titles. Thad Matta, Ohio State's coach, didn't—but he was still in his midforties. I was the guy with the bull's-eye on me.

didn't wall myself off from people in New Orleans. I know that some football coaches do that before their big games. Everybody operates like they're in a bunker, the head coach and his whole staff. Soundproof, no natural light, nothing but videotape and coffee and sandwiches. They come out into the open when they have to talk to the media, then scurry back into their hole.

I don't think that works in our game. All it would do is tie me up in knots, and my team would feed off me and they'd be in knots. We had our traditional big Final Four dinner a couple of nights before the semifinal, at Brennan's in the French Quarter. A few dozen friends were with me, some of my staff, my wife, my kids. Great food, great time.

I went to Mass in the mornings at the St. Louis Cathedral, which is one of the great things about being in New Orleans. It's a beautiful place, founded all the way back in 1721, the oldest Catholic cathedral in the country. I didn't buy a new suit for the Final Four. I brought two of them with me, suits that I'd worn a couple of times already during the season—one for the semifinal on Saturday and another, hopefully, for the final on Monday night.

Bob Rotella, the sports psychologist, was with us. He talked to the team as a group and to some guys individually who wanted to meet with him to get in the right frame of mind. His message was the same as mine—don't make it bigger than it is. It's a basketball game. It's the next game. You don't have to do any rah-rah stuff. You don't have to do anything extra. Just do what you're doing. Stay the course. You've been the best team all year and still are.

As a staff, we had to hear that same message. Whether it's the first game of the year or the last—whether we're playing Austin Peay or Louisville—don't change how you prepare. Don't watch more film than you normally would. Don't change the way you write on the whiteboard. Don't change the pregame routine. That sounds like a cliché, but it's one of the biggest things you have to do. If you get your kids too amped up, you're done.

Other than the nuts and bolts of the scouting report (Which guys on the other team shoot threes? Who crashes the offensive boards? If you have to foul, whom do you send to the line?), I don't want my players thinking about the other team. I don't want them thinking about "rivalry" games, and I definitely do not want them playing out of a sense of hate or anger.

The best players I've coached have a demeanor about them that never moves. They have a calmness. You can't read the score on their faces. Derrick Rose was like that. Anthony Davis was another. They'll get emotional, they'll play with fire, but their demeanor will never be one of rage or anger. Physiology-wise, rage and anger are related to fear. Hook a guy up to wires and look at his brain, and that's what you'll find.

There are coaches who will try to make their guys hate my team. We're winning that game every time. It works for them for a couple of minutes, maybe even a half, whatever. But when you play with a sense of rage, you don't respond well to being challenged. Once you lose a lead, miss a shot you should have made, don't get a call, all that rage turns to fear. The game's turning against you and you have no calm inner core to bring you back.

keep it really simple when I talk to the team before games. We go over our assignments. I tell them how I think the game will be played.

Louisville's rotation was mostly upperclassmen, including two seniors and a junior. They had physical strength and basketball know-how (which they would prove the following year, when essentially the same group would win their own national championship). "They'll try to bully you, foul you, and scrap with you," I said. "So you've got to be tougher than them. The game's going to be physical. So be prepared for it. Relish it. Love it."

Seventeen seconds in, we fell behind, 2–0. It was the only time we would trail the entire contest. We took a double-figure lead in the first half and maintained it through much of the second half until Louisville went on a run.

It was a pattern during the year, maybe our one weakness. There were stretches during games when we let teams off the mat—although to be fair, a good, well-coached team like Louisville is almost always going to make a run. You just have to survive it and then go on your own run.

With nine minutes to go, they tied us at forty-nine. I wasn't uncomfortable at that point. It was funny, but it just never entered my mind that we would lose. Our lead was gone, but I felt like we were in control.

We had not gotten much out of Michael to that point. He had gotten in foul trouble in the first half and played just six minutes. He was still out of sync. He had just missed a couple of bad-looking foul shots—one that he short-armed and left short, another that he clanked off the back rim.

With Michael struggling, it was fitting that the teammate who stepped up was Darius. With five minutes left, Marquis kicked it out to him on the right side and he hit a three-pointer. On the next trip down he drove it, got fouled, and sank two foul shots. Boom. We were back up nine points. That was pretty much it.

Later the media wanted to know about a play we'd made with one minute left, when Marquis drove the ball and floated an alley-oop to Anthony. The pass was a little wide, so Anthony reached back and grabbed it and slammed it home. It was spectacular looking but could be seen as a little risky at that point. The writers wanted to know if I had been upset that Marquis didn't just pull it back and let time run off the shot clock at that point.

No, I said. We're good when we attack. That's how we play. That's how we win.

If you looked at the box score of the Louisville game, you'd say that Anthony led us, which he did, posting the kind of ridiculous stat line that had become routine for him—eighteen points, fourteen rebounds, five blocked shots. He added two assists and a couple of times dribbled the ball up court against Louisville's press.

Rick Pitino was really gracious after the game. He wished me luck and said he hoped we brought a national title back to Kentucky. To the press he said, "Anytime you don't know whether a team is better offensively or defensively, you know you've got a great basketball team." He singled out Anthony. "He's the number one player in the draft," Rick said. "When you're playing against Bill Russell on the pro level, you realize why the Celtics won eleven world championships."

Anthony was asked what he had been shouting into a CBS camera after the game. Was he saying, "This is my state?"

No, he explained. He had said, "This is my *stage*."

When I think about this season, what always jumps out at me are some of the things that had probably never happened before. It's not always big stuff, and not everybody would notice it. I was proud of Anthony, of course, but when I look back on that game, I zero in on something else. We had six guys put up between six shots and nine shots, and not a single player with double-digit attempts. (Anthony got to eighteen points by hitting seven of his eight attempts from the floor, plus four out of his six foul shots.) It was the ultimate example of Players First—*plural*. Guys just didn't care about their own shots or stats. They were totally into what they were doing together. They knew we cared about them individually. I believe that gave them an even greater ability to care about each other—to be fully invested as teammates.

Somebody can go back and pore over box scores of Final Four games and see if there's ever been a winning team without a single guy putting up double-digit shots. I'm going to bet it hasn't happened very often—if ever.

We were matched up against Kansas on Monday night, which in the other semifinal had come from behind to beat Ohio State, 64–62. It had been the opposite of our win.

Kansas had been down thirteen points early and trailed just about the whole game.

I watched it on tape back at the hotel, not from a seat in the Superdome. After I coach forty minutes, I'm drained. I don't need to stay in the arena and watch another game. I told our kids they could stay if they wanted, but if I were them, I'd come back and rest up. I don't care how young you are—a two-day turnaround between games, with all the intensity of the Final Four, is really fast. It might feel like time is dragging, because of the anticipation of the championship game, but your body needs time to recover.

After our practice the next day, a radio guy came up to me and asked, "So, how do you feel being known as the best coach to never win a championship?"

I was thinking, *Is that an insult?* I didn't know what it was. People want to look at what you haven't accomplished yet and just assume you're unfulfilled. I think of myself as a husband, a father, a son, a friend, a mentor. I never look in the mirror and see my coaching record staring back at me. I never thought: *You poor slob, you'd be a lot happier if you could just get that done.*

But it's a story line, or maybe it makes some people feel better about their own lives. You know, *Hey, I haven't amounted to crap, but look at how miserable this other guy must be! He hasn't won one of those national championships.*

I got asked versions of that same question all weekend, and I'd just say, *Look, guys, I haven't been at Kentucky or these other schools that win national titles. I was at Massachusetts and Memphis.* Great places, and I loved them both. But UMass was good in basketball for two seasons back when Julius Erving played there. By the time I got hired, they were on a streak of ten con-

REASON TO SMILE: I loved playing for Clarion, a Division II school in Pennsylvania, where I started at point guard after transferring from the University of North Carolina, Wilmington.

THE GUYS AT CLARION: Senior year, I pulled off the feat of averaging 5.3 assists and 5.3 points a game.

IF IT MATTERS, WRITE IT DOWN: That's something my mom always told me. I also save stuff. My son, Brad, unearthed this list of goals I wrote down when I was twenty-six years old, and then posted it on his Instagram account without even telling me.

— Become a head coach before the age of 30.
— Win a national championship. By the 5th year.
— Be family oriented
    1. Family
    2. Social
    3. Basketball
— Be financially secure by age 35.
— Make others feel good.
— Care about the kids.
— Enjoy its only a game!
— Continue to grow and expand with the game... Learn & grow

ON THE SIDELINE AT UMASS: Can't tell here if I was upset at a referee or one of my players or maybe both.

1996 ALL-AMERICAN
MARCUS CAMBY
-UMASS-

COACH
JOHN R. WO

WITH THE WIZARD OF WESTWOOD: Marcus Camby with the late UCLA coach John Wooden at the banquet in which he received the John R. Wooden Award as the 1996 college basketball player of the year.

MAKING A POINT: I've coached many great point guards, none better than Derrick Rose, who played for me at Memphis. In his first three NBA seasons, he was NBA rookie of the year; an NBA all-star; and, finally, the league's most valuable player.

MY DREAM JOB: The press conference on April 1, 2009, when I was introduced as the new coach at the University of Kentucky. I hoped for the job when it came open a couple of years earlier, but it was worth the wait.

LOOKING ON: As my hiring was announced, from left to right, Connie Barnhart, wife of UK athletic director Mitch Barnhart; my son, Brad; daughter, Megan; and wife, Ellen.

PHEW!: We darn near lost the first game I coached at Kentucky, in Rupp against Miami of Ohio. After being down 18 points, John Wall hit this game winner at the end.

OLD-SCHOOL GUARDS: That's Eric Bledsoe with the ball, with John Wall behind him. They came to Lexington together, which surprised some people because both were considered point guards, but they meshed beautifully because neither needed the ball in his hands all the time.

BIG MAN, BIG PERSONALITY:
DeMarcus Cousins, with the headband, amid the "UK2K" celebration after we beat Drexel in December 2009 and became the first college program with two thousand victories.

PLEASANT SURPRISE:
Josh Harrellson could drive me nuts at times, but he got serious and became a big part of our success in 2010–11. Here he is blocking the shot of Ohio State all-American Jared Sullinger, whom he played to a standstill in our NCAA tourney victory.

DEFENSIVE STOPPER: We often counted on DeAndre Liggins to shut down the other team's best scorer, but that's not all he could do. I'm hugging him after his three-point shot in the waning moments against North Carolina iced the game that put us in the 2011 Final Four.

SAVED: We nearly got knocked out of the 2011 tournament in the first round against Princeton, but Brandon Knight, one of the most strong-willed players I've ever coached, hit this last-second shot to give us a 59–57 victory after he had been held scoreless for the first 39 minutes.

SENIOR NIGHT: Darius Miller, with his arm around his mother, Nicole Miller, celebrating one of the most illustrious careers in UK history. His father, Brian Miller, is just behind him.

NEVER GIVE UP ON A PLAY: That's an ethos of ours, and no one embodied it better than Michael Kidd-Gilchrist. Here, he was beaten by Kansas's Tyshawn Taylor near the end of the championship game. If Taylor scores, it gives Kansas hope, but Michael recovered, chased him down and made an unbelievable block.

ANOTHER HONOR: Anthony Davis picks up the Oscar Robertson award as the nation's top player, as voted by the U.S. Basketball Writers Association. His parents, Erainer and Anthony Sr., proudly look on, along with the "Big O" himself.

"THE STARTING SIX." The championship had six guys we considered starters—the five pictured here, including Darius Miller, who came off the bench, as well as Doron Lamb.

PURE JOY: The kids on our championship team had a love for each other that they expressed on the court by the way they played. Here, you see the culmination of their shared sacrifice and dedication to team.

JUST US: With my players in the moment right after the championship victory over Kansas, away from the press and the crowd. I'm doing some kind of celebration dance, which was very short in duration.

HOW SWEET IT IS: Anthony Davis, the MVP at the Final Four in 2012, cuts the net down at the Superdome after we defeated Kansas in the championship game.

VICTORY TOUR: We took the championship trophy all over Kentucky, because it seemed like the whole commonwealth wanted to see it and touch it. We got off the train in Midway on the way to Frankfort.

LONG WAY FROM MOON TOWNSHIP, PENNSYLVANIA: Here I am with the championship team at the White House, drawing a laugh from the nation's foremost college basketball fan.

BITTERSWEET MOMENTS: I'm proud when my players get drafted and begin their NBA careers, but I wish I had them longer. Here, in the spring of 2012, Anthony Davis, Doron Lamb, Terrence Jones, Michael Kidd-Gilchrist, and Marquis Teague announce they are putting their names in the draft.

NOT YOUR NORMAL LOCKER ROOM: This is the entrance leading to where our players dress before games at Rupp Arena. The collage of pictures shows Kentucky players currently in the NBA. The floor is the surface that we played on in our 2012 championship game at the Superdome.

OUR LEGACY: The big-time feel of the locker room is great, but the eight championship plaques serve to remind us of the high expectations that come with playing for Kentucky.

GIVING THANKS: Before our November 2012 game against Lafayette. A prayer, often led by a player, is part of our pregame ritual.

FREQUENT FLYER: My job requires a ridiculous amount of air travel, both with my team and in order to recruit. Here, I'm boarding the plane for Atlanta in 2012 for the Champions Classic matchup against Duke.

WHY, WHY, WHY? That's a normal response for coaches, because kids don't always do things the way you practiced with them or just instructed in a timeout. Here, I'm on the sideline during a loss in March 2013 at Arkansas.

DRAFT NIGHT 2013:
Nerlens Noel was the sixth pick in the June NBA draft, going to the New Orleans Pelicans, who immediately traded his rights to the Philadelphia 76ers for all-star point guard Jrue Holiday. If not for his knee injury, Nerlens would have been the top pick in the draft.

GREETINGS, BIG BLUE NATION: Kentucky fans get their first look at the 2013–14 team.

THE TWINS: By this time, I could tell them apart. That's Andrew on the left, and Aaron on the right.

TASTE OF THINGS TO COME: Julius Randle, on Madness night, soars for a dunk.

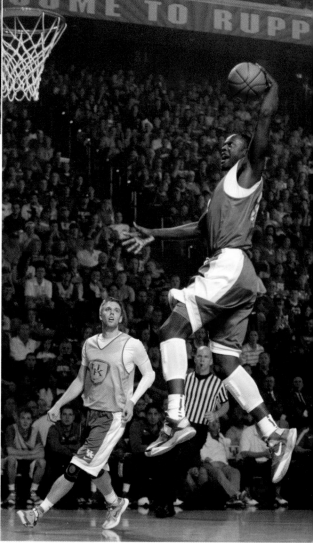

CONNECTIONS: Our best players often only stay one year, but they feel a part of the program and they come back. At Big Blue Madness in 2013, John Wall and Anthony Davis were among the former players looking on.

HOME AWAY FROM HOME: My office at the Joe Craft Center, overlooking our practice court. "Coach Your Team" is my reminder to concentrate on what we do, not our opponents. The bottles of bourbon on the window ledge are mementoes of one of our state's signature industries.

IN THE SHADOW OF GREATNESS: Our players and teams forge their own identities, but they do so amid constant reminders that they are part of a legendary basketball program.

SETTING THE RECORD STRAIGHT: DeWayne Peevy is the UK's deputy director of athletics and oversees media for the basketball program. The basketball on the desk commemorates my 500th coaching victory, and is the one the NCAA objected to because they keep a different count based on games that were "vacated."

secutive losing seasons. Memphis had more of a basketball tradition, but it was in a down cycle too, and it wasn't in a BCS
football conference—and those were the programs winning national championships.

Here I was in year three at Kentucky, and in my second Final
Four. I thought I was doing pretty well. Did I want to win the
game we had coming up? Yeah, obviously. Did I *need* to win a national championship to validate my career? No, I didn't, whether
you want to believe that or not. And I definitely didn't want my
players to think that.

If I was making it about me and my frustration level that I
had to win this national title, they'd know it. I told them, *If it
doesn't go well, I'll take responsibility, and if it goes well, you're
going to get the glory, so don't worry about it. You're the best team.
Just do what you do. You're not going to play perfect. If you break
down, just keep playing. The rest of it takes care of itself.*

O f course, as fate would have it, we were to play the team
and the coach that had come back and beaten my Memphis squad in the 2008 NCAA final after we'd lost a late lead. So
that made everything bigger.

It was the rematch of John Calipari versus Bill Self. Except
this time it was Kansas versus Kentucky, or as some were calling
it, Goliath versus Goliath. We were the two winningest programs
in the history of college basketball. Wilt Chamberlain played for
Kansas. Their first coach was James Naismith, who invented the
sport of basketball. (He is less known for being the only Kansas
coach in history to have a losing record.) Kansas went into that

game with three national titles, behind UCLA (eleven), us (seven at the time), North Carolina (five), Indiana (five), and Duke (five).

Was I haunted by what happened in 2008? No, I wasn't, but I'd be lying if I said I didn't think about it a little. How could I not? People kept reminding me.

Bill Self said before the game, "You know all the pressure is in their locker room." I understood why he would say that. We had been the best team all year, so we were supposed to win.

Steve Kerr, the former Chicago Bulls player, was doing commentary for CBS. Somebody told me later what he said about me. "He's been so loose, but I think it's been a little bit of an act." He was right. Part of coaching is acting. It's true of any kind of leadership, whether you're a CEO, an army general, or a father. Part of the job is that you don't reveal your own apprehensions. I don't ever go into games thinking we're going to lose, but of course I get anxious.

During the 1995–96 season at UMass, my good friend Mike Gottfried, the former Kansas and Pittsburgh football coach, now working at ESPN, called me and said, "You've got to loosen up and smile more." At the time we were 20-0, and his comment to me was, "You need to look like the happiest guy in the world. You've got to have everyone in the building, including your team, knowing you're having a ball. You've got to smile. You've got to laugh. You can't be out there looking sad or anxious."

From that moment on, I walked into every game smiling, laughing, talking to my staff, laughing at my staff even if what they were telling me wasn't funny. I had no idea if it had an effect until several months later when I was coaching the New Jersey Nets. We would bring in players whom we were considering for the draft for individual meetings, and one of the guys we met with was Jerome Williams of Georgetown. He had been on the team that we'd beaten by thirty that had Allen Iverson.

Jerome made a comment that kind of stunned me. He said, "How did you know you were going to win that game before it even started?" I looked at him and said, "What do you mean?" He said, "Our whole team looked down at you on the bench before the game and saw you smiling like you knew what was going to happen. We couldn't understand it." I just started laughing. Believe me when I tell you I had no idea we were going to win that game. But it was a mind-set. It was how I started to approach every game.

I write out an index card that I have with me during the games that has on it what we're going to do on offense, how we're going to guard certain things. It's basic. Here's what we do if they go zone. Here's how we break their press. Here are our baseline out-of-bounds plays. I have it with me to refer to, because in the heat of the moment sometimes you want it.

It's the same thing that goes up on our whiteboard for the players. It includes the other team's tendencies, but I don't overload them with that. I want them to focus on *our* stuff—what *we* do. I could have an assistant coach write it all out, but I do it myself. It goes back to what my mom said—the more you write it down, the more you remember it.

The team goes out on the court and does its layup drills and shoots, and then there comes a point when I have about fifteen minutes to myself. I'll be in there collecting my thoughts, but it's the worst time. The worst. There are still, like, thirty minutes before we tip off, and I have nothing to do but worry. I don't turn on the TV. I don't want to be seeing anything.

I have my rosary ring with me, so I always pray the rosary a little bit. Before a big game like that, I always say, *Good Lord, whatever you have in store for me, I'm fine with it. I will take responsibility if it goes wrong, and if it goes well, it will be about the players. We've done everything we're supposed to do to be prepared. However fate may intervene, just give me the strength to be there for these kids.*

You want to win with grace, and if you're a decent person you should be able to do that. You credit your opponents. You don't gloat. You teach your players to handle it that way. But you want to be able to accept losses without anger or bitterness, and it's not always easy when someone puts a microphone in your face seconds after the buzzer.

When we lost that game to Kansas in 2008, I wanted someone to foul at half court with ten seconds left so Kansas couldn't shoot a three-pointer and tie us. We didn't do that, and it might not have been possible.

The larger point is that it wasn't any of the kids' fault. When you have a nine-point lead with two minutes to go, the responsibility falls on the coach. I walked out of the locker room after talking to the team. Before the door closed, I was in front of cameras and microphones. My comment was, "When your team gets up nine points with two minutes to play, as a coach, you're supposed to win that game. I take full responsibility for the loss."

I never want one of my kids to be held publicly responsible

after a big loss. When I say that prayer, I'm thinking about those kinds of things. I ask for the strength and presence of mind, if need be, to serve as their protector.

Right before the Kansas game in New Orleans, I told the kids, "I'm feeling the butterflies right now but for no other reason than I want the country to watch this game and say, 'Damn, those guys have fun playing basketball. Look at them, they're having a ball.' " I told them to play hard, play for one another, and enjoy every minute of it.

I've said that I focus mainly on how our team plays, rather than on the opposition. If we play like we can, we win. It's that simple, and I feel that way every year because of the quality of the players we recruit. But obviously, I strategize with my assistant coaches on how to match up. That's why we watch all that videotape, to decide whom our players should guard, how they should guard them, and how we should attack on offense.

The big star for Kansas was Thomas Robinson, a strong player with a big heart and a lot of different ways to score inside. He finished second to Anthony Davis in most of the Player of the Year awards. Robinson was really good, but I thought he was undersized—a little shorter than his six-foot-nine program height—and not able to shoot over our inside players.

We decided to have Terrence guard him, not Anthony—which allowed Anthony to roam a little. If Robinson got to the hoop, Terrence could still challenge his shots. On the first possession we trapped Robinson with a second defender to make them think that's what we were doing. But most of the time Terrence played him straight up.

We wanted to force their offense back outside and make them beat us with jump shots. All teams have an identity, and that's not who they were. So the idea was to take them outside their comfort zone.

Rotella asked me before the game how we would counter if Kansas tried to slow the pace, and I said they wouldn't dare slow it down. Even if they succeeded, it would kill their recruiting. They recruit the same elite level of players that we do, often the very same guys, and those kids all want to play fast.

The weather in New Orleans that night was awful. Thunder and big bolts of lightning were in the area, which briefly dimmed the lights in the Superdome. It was weather fit for basketball Armageddon.

Right from the start, the game was like a full-out sprint, just like I thought it would be. And we got way out front. Ten minutes in we were up eight points. Four minutes later, on a three-pointer by Doron Lamb, we were up fifteen.

I had given Doron some special attention at our practice the day before, and then again at shootaround that day. He hadn't shot the ball that well against Louisville. I just kept saying to him, *You're getting twenty-five points in the final.* The more I talked, the better he stroked it. His shot looked beautiful. I started telling his teammates: *Doron's getting twenty-five. Just wait and see.*

Doron could play in different gears—fast, slow, and in between—which is part of what I meant when I wrote earlier about his feel for the game. When other guys were going crazy, he could just sort of fit himself in. With the fast pace I was expecting, and the physicality, I thought he would be able to drift to open space and get his shots, and I just wanted him in the right frame of mind to be able to make them.

We were ahead 41–27 when the first half ended—and Doron was leading us with twelve points. For Kansas, Thomas Robinson had six points on three-for-eleven shooting. He never stopped lowering his shoulder and bulling his way to the hoop, but every time he went up he was looking at a pair of long arms in his face—sometimes two pairs.

I think we frustrated him some. The old adage is that you go "right at" a shot blocker—take the ball into his body to neutralize him. He couldn't do that because Anthony wasn't playing him—but he was lurking nearby.

At halftime, Anthony had a surprising stat line. He had missed all four of his shots, a couple of them from point-blank range, and yet he was totally dominating the game. He had nine rebounds, four assists, and three blocked shots—and had probably made Kansas alter six other shots.

Anthony just figured it wasn't his night to score, and he genuinely didn't care. He told his teammates in the locker room, "Y'all score the ball. I'm just going to defend and rebound."

One thing I was worried about at that point was that I knew we should be up by more at halftime. We'd had them by eighteen points and then given up two layups, including one at the buzzer. It gave them hope. And I knew their coach was in there telling them that if they could get it close, we'd fold.

I told my guys, *You did great. I'm happy. Let's just go back out there and ball, but listen, you've got to keep your focus. You have to take care of the ball. And you can't give them any more easy baskets.*

———

Kenny Payne said of this team, "Their personalities were special. They loved each other. They had each other's backs at all times, and they hated the thought of losing." When players are that bonded, it breeds toughness. Terrence rolled his ankle in the second half. When I say that, I mean he rolled it all the way over. I saw him do it from the sideline and was like, *Oh my gosh, that is really ugly*. If you've ever turned your ankle like that, you know how it feels. You limp off, hope you didn't break or tear anything, get it taped up, then try to go back in the game when the pain subsides. Our trainer, Chris Simmons, was on the edge of his seat, but Terrence never even looked at the bench. He grimaced, then immediately got back on his feet and ran up the court.

Kansas had a hard time cutting into our lead. Just after the eleven-minute mark, Doron drifted to the left corner, Marquis found him, and he hit a three-pointer to put us up by thirteen points. On the next trip down, after we rebounded a miss, Doron accepted a handoff pass from Anthony near the top of the key. There was nothing to it. It's just what we teach— don't do Showtime, just make the simple play. Anthony rubbed the defender with a pick, Doron rose up for another three-pointer, and you knew it was good the moment it left his hands. That gave Doron six points in thirty-eight seconds—twenty points for the game—and put us up by sixteen with ten minutes to play.

We didn't unravel after that, but it got too tight for comfort.

We shot it horribly in the second half—27 percent. They hit a couple of three-pointers and finally got the margin under ten points with four minutes left. Two minutes later, our lead was down to five points. A couple of friends told me the announcers started talking about what had happened in 2008. I would have been surprised if they didn't.

We had stopped attacking, but that was my doing. Michael missed a layup. Somebody else missed a layup. We threw a cross-court pass that Michael ran down and saved just before it went out of bounds, which looked just like a play that had happened in the Memphis final. I didn't like that at all. (In the Memphis game, Kansas stole the pass and immediately hit a three-point shot, and they were off to the races after that. My Memphis kids were all jacked up. We called a time-out and one of them said to me, "We're okay." I said, "No, we're not okay.")

So now I saw all this stuff happening again, and just for a moment I thought, *Oh man, where is this going?* So I just decided to slow it down a little. I wanted more movement, more motion of the ball, so everybody could get a touch and relax. People later said, "You pulled back the reins. Why did you do that?" I did it because I wanted to make sure we won the game. You want to respond like a wiseguy and say, "Everybody's a coach, right?" They think they know your team better than you do.

But even Joe B. Hall said to me later, "Why'd you rein them in?" And he *is* a coach. But at that point we had a big lead. I had freshmen and sophomores on a big stage against seniors, and I didn't want this thing getting away from them before they even knew what hit them. Kansas had won its last regular-season game, against Missouri, by fighting back from nineteen points behind. They had done almost the same thing in the NCAA semifinal. I was sure Ohio State had thought they were going to be playing on Monday night, and the next thing they knew, they weren't. Kansas had climbed all over them.

When we first slowed it down, we banged the lead back up a couple of times. With the shot clock running down on one trip, Marquis just faced his man up at the top of the key and hit a three-pointer. There had been that point early in the season when Marquis wasn't in sync with what we wanted him to do. But he never lacked courage.

Kansas, though, kept chipping back at it, and we had some guys panicking a little bit. What finally ended it was a play by Michael. Kansas came out of a time-out with the ball, trailing by six points with a little more than a minute to play. If they hit any kind of hoop, they'd be right in it. If they hit a three-pointer, it would be down to a one-possession game, and I didn't know what would happen then.

I had Michael guarding their senior guard, Tyshawn Taylor, who set himself up on the right wing. As the ball came up the court, Taylor broke out toward the three-point arc. Michael went with him, then was totally beaten when Taylor put the brakes on and made a back-door cut to the basket. We had no help back there. Anthony was guarding his guy up near the foul line. Everybody else was spread around the perimeter.

By all rights, Michael was out of the play. Taylor was six foot two and one of the quickest kids in college basketball. He got a perfect bounce pass, crossed to the other side of the rim, and put up a reverse layup. But Michael didn't just turn around and yell "Help!" He knew there was no one back there. He chased him down, leaped, and blocked the shot. Taylor retrieved the ball but then kicked it out of bounds. Game over. Kansas had to foul—Marquis and Doron added four points from the line—and we won, 67–59.

I show a video clip of Michael's blocked shot to my current players—and will show it as long as I coach—because it's nothing but pure effort. The other kid beats Michael, but he absolutely refuses to accept it. To this day I don't know how he got back there to make the block. He just did.

There's one other important thing about this play. I told Michael in the time-out that Kansas was going to go back door, so he made a mistake when he let the kid go by him. But I tell kids all the time: *You're going to make mistakes; just play through them.* He didn't hang his head, even for a second. He just overcame his mistake with relentless determination and hustle.

Anthony Davis finally hit his first shot with five minutes left in the game. A 62 percent shooter during the year, he finished one for ten. With his four foul shots he scored six points. A lousy game for Anthony, right, and we just had to overcome it? Hardly.

Anthony was named the Final Four's Most Outstanding Player, which is probably another thing you will never see again—a kid with single-digit points and a 10 percent shooting percentage getting that award. But there wasn't even a doubt that he deserved it. He finished with sixteen rebounds and six blocked shots. His six assists were more than any player on either team. Without scoring much, he dominated the game.

I was really happy to see that recognized, because it was such a great validation of what we stand for. Do what you do. If you come up short in one area, your teammates will step up for you. It's not about your statistics; it's about what we do together.

———

On the podium at midcourt after the game, NCAA president Mark Emmert handed me the championship trophy. Jim Nantz of CBS, who was standing between us, asked me how it felt to finally have it in my hands. "Well, it's kind of heavy, to be honest with you," I said, and immediately handed it to our university president, Dr. Eli Capilouto.

I said just a few words about the game, passing along that the players were all over me for making them slow down. "I was just trying to get out of that gym alive," I explained. (Yeah, I know, the Superdome isn't best described as a "gym," but once a coach, always a coach. That's how we talk—the place you play basketball is a gym.)

I wish I could tell you that I loved being up there at that moment—the triumphant leader of the national champions, live on national television, finally at the pinnacle of his profession. But I didn't. A friend told me I looked sedated, which I wasn't, of course, but I felt uneasy and I didn't know why.

My whole career I wasn't a great player. I didn't play for one of the name coaches in our business. I wasn't a blue-chip player. I didn't have a leg up on anyone. My mom always told me that a person should dream bigger than their surroundings. This scene was huge—the setting, the moment, what we had achieved. Looking back on it, I think I felt overwhelmed and amazed. What the championship meant to me was that I could go about helping kids and families in the way I think is best. It validated how we do things. I had truly gone from the business of basketball to the business of helping families.

The focus on me didn't match what I was feeling inside. I was overjoyed for our players. And I was really happy about what it meant to our overall program—meaning what I can do for the kids who would come here in the future. If we had lost, maybe people would have had more success tearing that down—saying that you can't take these great players who might just stay a year and make it work for them and for the team. Those stories were already written. They just didn't get to print them.

CHAPTER 6

DECISION TIME

In my mind, our season doesn't end until the NBA draft in late June. During the season it's about team. From the moment our last game ends until the draft, it switches over to being about individual kids.

Some people think I only want players for one year—that I'm coaching them up and pushing them out. Nothing could be further from the truth. But I'm dealing realistically with the environment we're in. There's no use whining about the rules. (I will, however, put forward my ideas on changing them in the next chapter.) My responsibility is to deal with the situation intelligently, ethically, and in a fashion consistent with my Players First philosophy.

I want to recruit the very best players to Kentucky, as many of them as I can get. They are permitted to enter the NBA draft after one season with us, and if I do my job correctly, they will have that option. They'll be draftable. Hopefully, first rounders.

Lottery picks. I can't hold them back while they're with me and say, *Whoa, you're showing a little too much. You're getting too good, and I can't let that happen because I might lose you.* It doesn't work like that.

In a given season I'll have a minimum of three or four guys the NBA will want if the players decide to put their names in and make themselves eligible. Some years I'll have five, my whole starting lineup. Or maybe even seven or eight—my entire rotation.

Who should go? Who should stay? How do we work through the questions together and how can I help kids make the right decisions? And by that, I mean the right decisions for *them*. Not for me, the program, the university, or the Commonwealth of Kentucky.

The first thing I do is go out and get information on a kid's draft prospects. Is he going to be drafted at all? In what round? Is he a lottery pick? The ramifications are huge.

No player should give up his eligibility and scholarship if he might not even get drafted. If you want to go play in Europe, Asia, or South America, there's no rush. You can do that after you stay with us four years and get a degree.

But what if you're hovering somewhere between the first and second rounds? That's a tough one. If you make it into even the bottom of the first round, the thirtieth and last pick, you get a contract and guaranteed money—about $2.6 million over three years. That's not enough to set you up for the rest of your life—though many kids may think it is—but it's not nothing. It's a start. There's a good chance it's more money than anybody in your family has ever seen, and if you handle it properly, you can put it to good use.

But if you are the *thirty-first pick* overall—first selection in the second round—you're guaranteed nothing. Nada. You've got to make a roster. If you don't, you try to hook on to a team somewhere in the world that will pay you a salary.

I have the contacts among NBA scouts and executives to give a kid a pretty good idea where he's going to be drafted if he decides to leave us. Most coaches at major Division I programs can do the same. It's become a part of our jobs. But none of us are good enough to tell one of the in-between kids, with absolute certainty, exactly where he'll get picked.

I'll know if a player is, for example, somewhere between the twenty-fifth and thirty-fifth pick. If we're lucky, I might learn that a specific team with a late round one pick likes him and will pick him if he's still on the board. But that could come too late. At the point in April when a player has to decide if he's staying with us or turning pro, there are no certainties except for maybe just a handful of kids—the ones you know are going to be among the first two or three picks. (And even then you can be surprised. But at least you know those guys are getting drafted pretty high—and they'll have guaranteed money.)

Where in the first round a player is drafted is crucial. The number one pick, in most cases, is guaranteed about $13 million. After that it falls steadily slot by slot, and steeply. The tenth guy chosen is guaranteed $5.7 million—the twentieth, $3.4 million—as long as the team picks up the third-year option on their contracts. (If not, they could make less.)

So what is my approach with players? The first thing I do is give them the straight-up information—not what they're reading on all those online "mock draft" sites but what I know. It goes like this: *Here's how the NBA sees you. Here's what they like about*

you. Here's what they don't like. Here's what you can try to do be-
tween now and the draft—in your individual workouts, in inter-
views, and on the psychological tests—to address their concerns
and improve your position. I let them know where in the draft
they are likely to go, but it's a *range,* not an exact position.

I don't give them seven hundred pages of research. I don't
make it complicated, because it's not. The NBA scouts have seen
their games. They've been in our gym day after day watching
our practices. They have assembled the information to make
their judgments, and all I do is pass along to players, without my
own spin, how they are perceived. It doesn't matter what I think
or what the player thinks. There's no appeal process. (I will, to
the best of my ability, try to work the NBA executives and give
the most flattering possible account of my players when I'm
asked about them, because I want them to be drafted as high as
possible.)

A player's family, friends, and associates are almost always
giving him a best-case scenario. *You're a lottery pick. You're going*
to make X amount of money. You'll be an NBA all-star and cash in
big time on your second contract. Great. I hope it all happens.

But one of my most important roles is to give them the *worst-*
case scenario. For the kids who could fall into the second round,
Can you handle that uncertainty? Are you willing to live with the
consequences if it doesn't work out and you end up in a foreign
country where people speak a language you don't understand—and
the next spring you're sitting by yourself, watching on TV, as your
former teammates are playing the Final Four and having a ball?

The answer from the player is usually something like *"Oh*
yeah, Coach Cal, I could do that. It wouldn't bother me." Really?

You're sure about that? I'll tell you what, after we're done why don't you go home and keep thinking about it a little more, just in case you have any doubts.

The kids who legitimately think they could be lottery picks, but it's not a sure thing, I ask: *What if you end up as the fourteenth selection when you thought you might be the fifth guy picked? Whatever money you planned on making, it just got cut in half. You lost five million dollars while you were sitting there waiting for your name to get called. You're okay with that?*

For players we know are going to be drafted in the first round—but probably somewhere either middle or late first round—we have to talk about what happens if they decide to come back to Kentucky. *What is the likelihood of improving your draft position? What do you have to do—in terms of improving your body and your skills—to make that happen? If you feel in your heart you've maxed out in terms of what you can show the NBA, be honest about it. I might not agree, but you're the one who has to be willing to put in the work. Just because you're a year older doesn't automatically make you a year better.*

I also have to tell kids about the risks of *staying,* because there are some. What if you come back and for whatever reason, your NBA stock plummets? It shouldn't happen—and has not happened in our program—but it can and sometimes does. If I'm being straight up and honest, then I have to acknowledge that there is a possible downside.

I don't talk to my players only about their likely slot in the draft but also about what comes after they enter the league. The kids who leave me may get guaranteed first-round money, but that does not mean they get a guaranteed spot on an NBA roster.

They could end in the NBA's Development League, commonly called the D League.

Those franchises are in places like Bakersfield, California; Erie, Pennsylvania; and Boise, Idaho. You're making money, but in every other regard it's a step down from playing at Kentucky. Everything here is big time, bright lights. It's fun, the arenas are packed, the weight room and locker rooms and other facilities are first class. The D League is not that. Our kids have been a little spoiled in Lexington, with chartered jets to road games and so forth. In the D League, you're traveling commercial, I'll tell you that. It's not going to kill them, but it's probably something they ought to know about.

I tell them that the D League is a possibility. In fact, it may be a *probability*. I've had some really good players put their time in with the D League, and there's no shame in it. But they have to consider how they'd feel about giving up another season with us in order to spend, say, the months of January and February in Sioux Falls, South Dakota.

Another thing: *Are you ready to be the CEO of your own company? Are you ready to say no to people who have been over top of you your whole life? Are you ready to say no to your mom and dad, your sister, your brother, guys who have coached you and helped you? Because it's your career and your money, and it only works if you're the one ultimately in charge of it. You get people to advise you, but you're the decision maker. If you're not ready to do that, then you're not ready to go.*

I might have a series of conversations with players, but we don't sit down and talk fifty times. They have other people they're consulting—their parents, former coaches, people in their communities who have taken an interest in them. Some of these people may give them bad advice, based on their own selfish interests, but I don't assume everyone is telling them the wrong stuff. That would be pretty arrogant on my part.

The player has to sort it all out, as hard as that is. I'll be a sounding board, but I can't put myself in charge of his whole circle. Nor will I help him pick an agent. I make it very clear: *I'm not getting involved in telling you how to run your business affairs.* If something goes wrong, I don't ever want them looking back and saying I was part of it.

I have people who advise me about money whom I trust, and that's what my players have to find. If they ask me what I think about a certain agent, and I have some knowledge about the guy, I won't hesitate to share what I know. But I'm not steering them to anyone. It's just not the right thing for me to do, and it doesn't lead to anything good.

I absolutely *do,* however, talk to them about the overall subject of money. In fact, after a player tells me he's definitely going to the NBA, he hears my "money talk." The gist of it is this: *Put your first million dollars away and don't touch it. Put it in a stock fund, fairly conservative, and have a professional manage it.*

In seven to ten years, under normal conditions, it will double. After that you can just keep on letting it grow. But if you need it, you can draw $150,000, $200,000 a year out of it and still keep the principal. Could you live the rest of your life that way if you needed to? You should be able to.

The reason I tell them to put a million away is that after they sign the first contract, they're going to buy themselves an expensive car. How do I know that? Because they've been talking about it since I first met them. And they'll buy a car for their mom, too. A whole bunch of money will go to taxes, and a big chunk will go to the agent.

What looks like a big pot of money has a way of disappearing. They're already thinking about that second contract from their first day in the league. In the NBA, that's where the big money is. But what if it doesn't happen? What if they get hurt, or they're just not as good as everybody thought? That's why I tell them: PUT THAT MONEY AWAY. A million bucks. Don't put your hands on it. Just know it's there.

Obviously, I'm not looking at their bank accounts. But some of them have come back and said they took my advice, and I've had moms tell me the same thing and thank me for advising their sons to do it. None of us knows what the future holds. I want to believe that every one of the kids we've sent off to the NBA is going to succeed. But I also want them to have that nest egg to fall back on just in case they don't.

CHAPTER 7

THE TROUBLE WITH ONE AND DONE

Basketball fans of a certain age remember the name Spencer Haywood. He graduated from high school in 1967, then played a year in junior college followed by one season at the University of Detroit. After that, he signed with the Denver Rockets, at the time part of the old American Basketball Association. He was really good right away, averaging thirty points and almost twenty rebounds a game in his rookie year.

That next season, the NBA's Seattle SuperSonics signed him, but the league tried to block it because back then, an incoming player had to play four years of college ball (or had to be four years past his high school graduation). The Sonics owner sued, and the case went all the way up to the Supreme Court.

The justices ruled that Haywood should be allowed to play, and that was the end of pro basketball's ability to keep players in college—or, for a time, even make sure they went at all. Moses

Malone went straight from high school to the ABA in 1974, then two years later (after the leagues merged) to the NBA. He's in the Hall of Fame and was voted into the NBA's list of top fifty all-time players. Two other players—Darryl Dawkins and Bill Willoughby—came straight out of high school in 1975. They had decent pro careers but probably would have been better off if they'd spent some time playing in college.

Then it stopped for a couple of decades. Players were leaving college early for the NBA, but no one came straight out of high school until Kevin Garnett in 1995. Some great players followed Garnett's route—Kobe Bryant, Tracy McGrady, LeBron James, Dwight Howard—but so did a number of guys who were busts. They gave up their college eligibility and either did not do well in the league or never made it at all.

The NBA didn't like taking players straight out of high school because it couldn't be sure what it was getting. With someone like LeBron or Kobe, it was obvious that they had ridiculous talent. But with others, it was harder to tell. And they had never been tested against competition above a high school level. These days, even if a player goes straight from his freshman season of college ball to the NBA, scouts have seen him play against opponents who are twenty-two, twenty-three, sometimes even twenty-four years old. They have a sense of his physical strength, his maturity, his basketball IQ in a way that wouldn't be possible if they'd seen him only against high school and AAU competition.

Also, and this is important, most of the players coming straight from high school were total unknowns to basketball fans. That was not good for the NBA, which gets an enormous marketing benefit from college basketball, because most of the high draft picks entering the league in the fall were just all over TV the previous spring in the NCAA tournament. (LeBron was an exception, because his *high school* games were nationally televised.)

When John Wall got drafted in Washington, Anthony Davis in New Orleans, or DeMarcus Cousins in Sacramento, 90 percent of the fans of those teams already knew of those kids and were excited to see them play. They had an identifiable brand. They were Kentucky players. The same goes for players from Duke, Kansas, Michigan State, and all the other schools that regularly make deep runs in the tournament. The NBA loves that and doesn't pay a penny for it. How great is that for the NBA?

The owners want players in college, the more time, the better. They get a more finished product, more known to them and to basketball fans nationwide. The current system we have was the result of a sort of tug-of-war among the league, the agents, and the NBA players' association. The agents, who have a lot of say in the players' union, want them in the NBA as soon as possible so they can get that first contract—and the clock starts ticking to the more lucrative second deal. They figure that kids can never make up the $2 million or $3 million they would have made when they were playing in college instead.

The compromise that got hammered out in the 2005 collective bargaining agreement put us where we are now—at "one and done." Players cannot go to the NBA until one year past their high school graduation. So they come to us. They play one season. And then the best of them leave.

I've made it work for the teams I coach—and for the players—as best I can. But I don't like it one bit. Some people say I'm renting players or I'm working the system. Let me make this very clear. I want to coach players for four years. Very few of the young players are truly ready for the rigors of the NBA. Some weren't even all that terrific in the college game. They get drafted on pure potential, because NBA teams are terrified of passing on a player who might—three or four years down the road—be an all-star.

But in the meantime, a lot of kids are playing above their heads, sitting on the bench, or getting sent out to the D League. All but a handful of them would benefit from more time playing college basketball, more class time, more time on a college campus.

I'm not too modest to say they'd benefit from more time with me. I'm a coach. I'm a teacher. I'm a mentor. I love what I do and think I help kids. I give them everything I can in a year, but I think I could do more in two years.

Notice I didn't say that if we changed the one-and-done rule it would be *better for college basketball.* I hear people talk like that and sometimes I want to laugh. It sounds so high-minded, but what's college basketball? Can anybody tell me? Is it something unto itself that exists on its own, with a soul and a heart that beats? Is college basketball just a spawn of the NCAA? Or when we say that we care about "the good of the game," are we talking about its history? Are we trying to answer the eternal question, "What would Phog Allen do?"

I don't think it's any of these things. For me, college basketball is the people in it—primarily the players. I do care about the history and tradition and doing what's right. I care deeply. But in my mind, the point of keeping the game healthy—of being responsible custodians, if you want to put it in those terms—is to benefit the young men playing the game now, and those who will come into it in the future. I want us to do the right things *for them*. And we're not doing that right now.

What I propose is not that radical, nor should it be difficult. All that it would require is that the NBA come together with the players' association and agree that no player comes into the league until at least two years after his high school class has graduated—or, at the very least, change the incentives so that players are strongly encouraged to stay. (Right now we do the opposite.)

The agents are the ones most opposed to this. Some things could be built into this arrangement to bring them along—most important, a provision that for a top category of college players, NBA rookie contracts would be one year shorter for those who stay in college two years.

The benefit for our players would be greater than most people realize. When we sign a kid out of high school, he's on our campus just about immediately after his high school graduation—taking college courses and beginning to accumulate credits. By the next May, if he has done what he's supposed to do, he has more credits than a normal freshman. Across college basketball, players follow the same pattern. That's why you see some players categorized as seniors (and sometimes even juniors) in terms of their NCAA eligibility who already have their degrees and are taking graduate courses.

So what happens if we require a player to stay two years? He has already taken summer courses right after high school. He goes through his freshman year. He takes more summer courses the following summer. Then he completes his sophomore year. So even if he puts his name in the draft and goes to the NBA, he should be about one year from graduation. He's close to fully educated—a year from his degree, not three years.

If we get them to stay through their sophomore season, we can get them that far down the road academically. If a kid wants to come back and finish—and we have had great success getting our former players to do that very thing—he can do it if he's close. In the meantime, he has been on a college campus another year. He's grown up a little bit more. His body and mind are more ready for pro basketball.

If he comes back and earns his degree, what's the ripple effect? He has shown his own kids—and everyone else—that he's a famous guy who values education. He came back and got it done.

Some people think players don't care about the academic aspect. That's crap. We get kids with a range of abilities in the classroom, but nearly all of them want to do well. Some tell me when they get here that they don't like being students, and then they end up changing their minds. Willie Cauley-Stein is a great example. He *hated* going to class and doing his schoolwork, or that's what he thought.

He would have been a first-round pick for sure if he'd left after his freshman year, but he stayed—partly because he'd decided he liked being in college. I think I helped Willie along by putting him in my unofficial book club. We picked out a book every two weeks, read it, and then sat down in my office and had a discussion about it. "You're going to learn to love reading because you're going to read," I told him, and that turned out to be the case. One of the books was *God Never Blinks*, essays by a *Cleve-*

land *Plain Dealer* columnist named Regina Brett, who is a single mom and a cancer survivor. It's the sort of material I like to put in front of my players, who so easily get wrapped up in their own troubles. When *Sports Illustrated* interviewed him, he told them, "That book gave me a different perspective on life."

In discussions about the NBA, I start by listening to the player. When I got to Kentucky, I assumed Patrick Patterson would not be one of my players—that he would go into the draft. He surprised me when he said he would stay. I tested his reasoning. I said, "You're twenty-two years old, you're going to be drafted in the twenties, maybe as low as seventeen or eighteen. What do you want to gain?" (Another way of asking: What is your "why"?)

He said, "I'm going to graduate in three years. I've never been to the NCAA tournament. And you're going to teach me how to play out on the floor. I've been playing with my back to the basket."

I was like, *Good, we're done.* That reasoning made perfect sense to me. It wasn't what I thought I would hear when I sat down with him, but I was thrilled I would have Patrick on the team and was really happy that he was so clear about the reason for his decision.

After Patrick became a very solid NBA player with the Toronto Raptors, he talked about the decision to stay that additional season at Kentucky. "It opened up my game," he said. "Had I not stayed, I would have come out as a six-foot-eight center. I would have had to start from scratch when I got to the NBA."

There are people in academia who despise athletes. I'm not giving away a big secret when I say that. It's been the case for a hundred years, since Harvard and Yale were playing football in leather helmets. They just assume that if you play a sport, you're dumb and you have no rightful place within the university. Well,

Brandon Knight was a straight-A student. Alex Poythress might have struggled with consistency on the court his freshman season, but in the classroom he earned a 4.0 grade point average. You're telling me those kids don't deserve to be on campus?

Let me stop right here for a moment. It's easy for people on the outside to say that once they're here, players should just stay in school, whatever the rules are that we set. Get your education. You'll always have it. Impossible to argue with, right?

But I have put players into the NBA over the last two decades, young men I coached at UMass, Memphis, and Kentucky, who have earned—or will earn, just through the 2013–14 NBA season—close to $400 million. In the next couple of years, with the seventeen Kentucky players drafted since 2010 starting to sign their lucrative second deals, that total will spike significantly. When you also include their endorsement money, their earnings will reach or exceed $1 billion.

Just as an aside, the Web site SB Nation put together a panel of voters and compiled a list of the projected top one hundred players in the NBA in 2017. Take it for what it's worth, but twelve of the players on the list are guys I coached in college—ten at Kentucky, two at Memphis. Some were still just getting settled into the league and finding a place—like Terrence, Enes, and Eric. Two of them, Andrew Harrison and Julius Randle, had yet to even play their first game for me. Nine of the top fifty were my players. Anthony came in at number seven; Derrick at five.

I don't measure my own value by the amount of money I make, and I don't judge anyone else that way, either. I hope the kids I coach make their lives about a lot more than their big contracts. But money is not *unimportant,* especially when it goes to kids and families and communities that are in need.

People jumping at money is not particular to basketball. Or sports. It's part of the human condition. It's what most people do, given the opportunity. And by the way, we're not talking about money that's out there for getting involved in something criminal. No, what these kids are faced with is having a big pile of money put in front of them for something they already love— *playing basketball.* Are you kidding me? A couple of years ago one of our U.S. senators from Kentucky, Mitch McConnell, asked me how many of our players were going into the NBA draft. I said six of them were. He said to me, "Do you realize you're creating more millionaires than a Wall Street firm?" We both laughed. It's not technically true, but what he said made me feel an even greater weight of responsibility, because of the amount of wealth I'm helping create for kids and their families.

Nobody makes a big deal out of it when baseball players turn pro right out of high school. I don't remember an uproar when Tiger Woods left Stanford for the PGA Tour. Neither Bill Gates nor the late Steve Jobs made it all the way through college. We've had *swimmers* turn pro and pass up college. Teenage girls play pro tennis and take their high school courses with private tutors while they're on tour, and very few continue on to college.

If gifted, NBA-quality basketball players are to come to college at all—and then to stay an additional year—we have to take care of them properly. Part of that means they have to know they are protected if they get injured. We're not keeping them for four years. Those days are gone. My point is that there's a middle ground.

Understand this about one and done: It is an NBA rule that's in the labor agreement with the players' association, which means we at the college level have no control over it whatsoever.

The owners are comfortable with one year and would like it to go to two. The players' association is somewhat uncomfortable with one year and would like it to go back to the high school rule.

What's that tell me? The rule may never change.

If it doesn't, what can we do to make sure that we are taking care of the kids who stay in school a year and encourage them to stay longer—if it's in their best interest? What can we do to slow this train down for the vast majority of players, who would be better off with at least one more year of college?

Let's start with something simple: Pay their disability insurance. You may say, *Pay their disability insurance? Isn't that paid for?* Nope. That insurance covers the player if he incurs a career-ending injury and never plays basketball again. To qualify for the insurance, the player's name is put before a committee that tells him whether he can be insured or not. He must be a first-round prospect in order to qualify for anywhere from $500,000 to $20 million of insurance.

Here's the kicker: If a player is eligible for the insurance, he must take a loan and pay it back after he enters the NBA—*or* even if he never makes it. It's not cheap, by the way. Per $1 million of coverage, the premium is approximately $5,000. So do the math. Five million dollars' worth of insurance that guards against a career-ending injury—a fraction of what a player would make over a career—costs $25,000. For every year he stays in college.

Why wouldn't the NCAA or the schools pay for this? Do you really think a kid is going to stay in school and have a $100,000 bill to pay back, or would this encourage him to leave early?

We should approach the NBA and see if it will help us encourage kids to stay in school longer. If a player is a part of the cohort of fifteen to seventeen players a year who get the insurance, and he chooses to stay in school an extra year, would the NBA consider taking a year off his rookie contract?

It's a good deal all around. The player gets to his second deal faster. He's more ready by the time he enters the league, so he should be more valuable. He's closer to his degree. The college game becomes more talent driven. The NBA gets a better-rounded player who is more marketable and more mature. And NBA veterans are not losing jobs to one-year guys who aren't ready and who are eventually not going to make it in the league.

This is common sense stuff, not that difficult. When a player comes to me now and he's considering the NBA, if I think the time is right for him, I tell him to go ahead. In good conscience, it's the only thing I *can* say.

The NCAA is not going to initiate reform; it has to be pushed. I thought for a time that I was making some progress toward change. I had a good working relationship with Billy Hunter, the former executive director of the players' union—the National Basketball Players Association. He came to Lexington, and we talked through a lot of the issues around one and done. I don't know if we agreed on everything, but we were having good conversations. I put him on the phone with other college coaches.

He trusted me. I think a lot of guys in the NBA trust me. And I think we could have gotten somewhere with me as the point man, but the NCAA was not interested in my help. The message I got, between the lines, was *No, not you. Not Calipari. We don't want him involved.*

They're holier than thou. There was talk of putting NCAA basketball in line with the "baseball rule"—which is that high school baseball players either go right into pro ball or, if they choose college, have to stay for three years.

That's just stupid for our game. I don't have another word for it. The NBA doesn't want high school kids, and it doesn't have a whole minor-league system from rookie ball up through triple A to develop them. The baseball rule would keep some kids in college basketball for three years who want to be in the NBA—without improving their situation in any way. (Baseball, by the way, doesn't pay most signees anything like what the NBA pays; if it did, you'd see a revolt against the "baseball rule" by baseball players.)

The baseball rule has kids coming right out of high school. My major concern is this: Do we want a generation of kids, many of them urban kids, who don't strive for education? Are we encouraging them to go directly to the NBA out of high school? You have to understand that the NCAA has raised academic standards for admissions and has made it more difficult for student-athletes to catch up if they've fallen behind as a sophomore, a junior, or even a freshman. Now, instead of being concerned about academics, two thousand to three thousand sophomores are worried about going to the league, not about academics. By the time they figure out they don't have the talent, it's too late academically. Now what? Too bad? It's not my son? They should have known better? I don't want to be a part of that.

The most recent thing that happened is that I was invited to serve on the board of the National Association of Basketball Coaches. Lots of great coaches are on the NABC board, and many others have been in the past. Twenty years as a head coach, three Final Fours, and a national championship, and it's the first time I've been asked. It's an honor. And it gives me a platform to keep pushing on issues that I care about.

But I'm pretty sure they knew what they were getting when

they asked me. I'm not going to shut up. I want to press a lot of stuff. I've already started. I want to get a small group of coaches together—high-profile guys—and say, *Let's look creatively at this. If the goal is to keep kids for at least two years, what makes that happen?*

One possibility is to not *require* two years in college but encourage it in various ways. For example: For the players projected as high draft choices, we could set up a system where they can get a loan against future earnings. It's transparent, all above board. They have to pay it back.

If a kid is eligible for this "insurance loan" and there is a death benefit of $100,000 on the policy, why wouldn't his family be able to get a separate loan from the bank based on future earnings? In a year or two this young man is going to be worth anywhere from $5 million to $15 million or more. His family should be allowed a $50,000 loan that they would pay back later. If he graduates, the loan should be forgiven.

The other option for these kids and their families is to go underground and take a loan from an agent or someone connected to an agent. We've all seen this in past NCAA cases. Agents or other people get their hooks into players. Not only does the kid now owe somebody, but he's also beholden because the guy who lent him the money is the keeper of a dark secret. He and the kid are in a dirty deal together.

The guy who gave the kid money knows that an NCAA violation has occurred, so he can hurt the player, the school, the coach, and the kid's teammates. That's a lot of power to have. He opens his mouth and the whole thing can come crashing down. So now you have a player who is in debt—*and* in fear. That's what we do to kids.

What bothers me the most is when people say that these families, even if they could get the loan themselves, would still take money from agents and others. Do you know how dumb a statement that is? Because the money they get from an agent or others is not a grant—it's a loan, and at some point their son has to pay that back with interest. If you think these families want to be indebted to anyone, then you haven't been in their homes recruiting their children.

Would the player be taking a chance that he would have to pay the money back if he didn't make the NBA? Yes, and his family would have to take that into consideration. But I think it should be an option.

In the NCAA offices, they can talk about their reams of regulations and lofty ideals and just about the last dying notions of "amateur" athletics anywhere in the world. What I'm talking about is the street-level reality.

The more we help players—and put a safety net under them that provides reasonable benefits—the more we get in the way of this kind of stuff. Every one of my scholarship players wants to go to the NBA, and many think they are ready from the first moment they set foot on campus. That's natural. They're young and full of themselves. We have to be given more tools to pull them back in when it's necessary.

I don't want kids feeling deprived at the same time they're performing within a billion-dollar enterprise. I don't want them feeling like criminals because they live in a world where somebody is always flashing an improper benefit in front of them.

It's all part of what chases them into the NBA. As a player, you've got to be ready when you make the jump. You get one bite at the apple. If you go too early, you may recover. But there's a good chance you won't.

There is one more suggestion I have to improve the current one-and-done system, as long as we have to live under it, and give players more information and a better basis for making decisions. The funny thing is, I've already done this on my own.

After the 2011 Final Four season, we ran a "combine" on our campus similar to what NCAA Division I football teams do—a showcase for our players, as well as an opportunity for them to get a realistic picture of how the NBA viewed them. We had more than twenty NBA teams come to campus and watch our players being put through the same workouts that the teams give prospective draft picks at their practice sites. They then had individual meetings with our players.

Wouldn't this close contact with the pros encourage more kids to leave early? Actually, no. It was after this combine, and after their meeting with the NBA, that two of our players—Doron Lamb and Terrence Jones—decided they would be better off coming back to Kentucky.

If we had done that with Archie Goodwin in 2013, might he have possibly come back? We'll never know that because of a new rule that the players have to make a decision by mid-April. The new date is a couple of weeks after our season ends, while our classes are still going on. It's too soon, and it rushes our kids unnecessarily. Under the old calendar, they could work out for NBA teams while they were still coming to a decision. Not anymore.

From the moment the kid makes a decision, he cannot reverse himself. What if the kid doesn't get drafted? What if he made a mistake? Too bad.

My suggestion is that each conference should have a combine. It's entirely up to the player if he's interested. If he's undecided about declaring for the draft, he probably goes and gets more information. If he's already a high pick and set on the NBA, and he has nothing to gain, he doesn't. If he's not interested in coming out, then obviously he just skips the whole thing and returns to school.

There will always be kids who hear what they want to hear and make ill-advised decisions. I'd like to be able to say that we did our job, that for those players and families who wanted to do their due diligence, we gave them the information they needed.

Some people ask, *Why do you recruit all these one-and-done players, and why would you want a whole team of them?* There's been criticism in the press and from retired coaches, as well as a quiet disapproval from some current coaches. The insinuation, I guess, is that I'm doing something wrong.

To be honest, I don't get it. But how about this? If college coaches are so against one and done, why aren't more of them speaking out and trying to end it? Why isn't it a cause? Remember, now, I'm not the only one recruiting these kids.

Could it be that some of them don't *want* me to have these kids for more than a year? Imagine some of my lineups if you combined a couple of classes, if, say, John Wall and DeMarcus Cousins, as sophomores, had played with the next year's group. Or if the guys from the 2011–12 championship season had stayed on to mentor the guys who followed them? Best for some of them to start their pro careers, right, if you're trying to beat Kentucky?

I don't know how to recruit a different level of player. I can't go out there and say, *All right, I've got my really good guys, so now I'm going to sign up some sort of good guys. Great! I've got them signed on the dotted line, so now let me top off this class with a really average player—a six-foot-five power forward, let's say, a little overweight. Can't go to his left, but a heck of a kid!*

There's no way I'm intentionally recruiting a player because I know the NBA won't want him after a year or two. And I'm not making a two-tiered system where I say to one kid, *Yeah, you can go if you want—but you, over there, I'm getting in your way. I'm not going to showcase you properly. I'm going to praise this other kid to the NBA scouts, but I'm going to whisper to them that they'd be making a big mistake if they chose you. Because, after all, I can't have my whole team leaving.*

It would create problems in my locker room, and it's just not right. We put our team together in the fall, and we go to war against one another in the practice gym. We play our season, then let the chips fall where they may.

One of the great downfalls of the current system is that some of the kids who put their names in the draft don't really want to go. They do so with a great degree of sadness. They'd stay if we made some changes. "I didn't want to leave this place," DeMarcus Cousins said after he declared for the draft. "It was a hard decision. If I did come back, I could get hurt. Anything can happen. My stock is high right now."

A reporter asked him if I had "pushed" him out. "He told me it's my time to go," DeMarcus replied.

And that was true, I did tell him that. He was the fifth pick in the 2010 NBA draft. If he'd stayed would he have been the third pick the next year? The first? I'm not sure. He got about $9 million in guaranteed money from the Sacramento Kings and, with the way he has performed, put himself in line for a second contract in the vicinity of what John Wall, the first pick in that same draft, signed—$80 million over five years. He reportedly got $60 million over four years. One thing I'm really proud of is that both of these young men, immediately after agreeing to their deals, donated $1 million to charity.

Don't get me wrong, if DeMarcus had wanted to come back, I would have loved to coach him again. But with all the uncertainties, I couldn't advise him to do that.

When our guys leave, they die over it. They know what they're giving up. I said to DeMarcus what I tell them all: *You're entering a man's world. You're not going to have the same relationship you had with me and my staff. You're an asset to your franchise. They're not looking at it any other way. That's what it is, and if you don't perform, they'll put another asset in there. If you do perform, they'll be real nice to you. The relationship you have here with your teammates—where you are your brother's keeper—it won't be like that. They've got families. A wife and kids. They've got a business manager and an agent. They've got their own friends to deal with. They're not dealing with you. So you go your way, and they go their way, and then you come back and practice. It's a business.*

Michael Kidd-Gilchrist was among the players who came back to Lexington for the annual alumni game in the summer of 2013. "In college it was a brotherhood," he said. "Now it's just grown men. I'm growing up fast."

The whole issue of whether or not players will declare for the NBA draft can become a distraction if you let it—and right when your team is playing the most important games of the season. I got asked about it by the media right after we beat Louisville in the 2012 semifinal game, with the final looming in forty-eight hours. The insinuation, as always, was that it was somehow bad if we won a national championship and a bunch of my freshmen left.

All I could say was that it's not my rule and it's not my players' rule. You recruit players as good as the ones I have, and this is the position you'll be in. If my kids leave, is it worse than if kids from Duke or North Carolina leave? Is that what you're telling me? Apparently it is, because those coaches don't get asked about it like I do. I also reminded everyone that we were the most efficient team in the country. We rebounded, defended, hit a high percentage of our shots. We weren't just bringing in future NBA kids for a stopover and rolling balls out on the floor at practice. We were coaching them.

In the postgame locker room after we beat Kansas, I told the guys to enjoy the moment without thinking about the future. When reporters ask if you're going to the NBA, I said—which they surely would—just smile and tell them that it's a question for another day. You've got a month to make a decision, and right now it's not even in your mind.

The one player we obviously knew we would lose from the NCAA championship team was Darius, our senior. He was the epitome of everything we stand for—sacrifice, being a good teammate, playing the right way. When we were invited to the White House that May, he was the one we asked to present President Obama with a commemorative Kentucky jersey and championship ring.

Darius was a second-round pick of the New Orleans Pelicans (forty-sixth overall), made their roster, and spent a little time in the D League while getting into fifty-two NBA games—which is not bad at all for a second-round pick. I'm absolutely confident he'll have a solid pro career because his NBA coaches are going to value the same winning qualities that he displayed at Kentucky.

Doron, who had considered leaving after his freshman season, declared for the draft and was picked by Milwaukee in the second round, forty-second overall. His mind was made up. Just as with Darius, I was a little disappointed that he didn't sneak into the first round, but Doron, too, looks like he'll stick in the league if he keeps working at it. He has that shot-making ability—and the sophistication to his game—that was evident from day one at Kentucky.

Terrence Jones went to Houston as the eighteenth pick in the first round, probably somewhere around the same place he would have gone if he'd come out after his freshman season. That's how it works sometimes. The NBA projects what players will become three, four, or five years down the road. When the scouts observe you for another season in college, it may just solidify their opinion. (That does *not* mean, however, that the player wouldn't be better off staying and preparing himself that extra season.)

Terrence is one of the main reasons I warn my players they may put in time in the D League. He is really gifted physically, with high-level basketball skills, but he was twenty years old when he started with the Rockets, and they had a good roster. He spent a lot of his year with Rio Grande Valley Vipers, which I guarantee you is not what he had in mind when he left us. He played in just nineteen regular-season NBA games. But he did well when given the opportunity, was included on the Rockets' postseason roster, and got into a couple of play-off games—which were good omens. Now he's a starter for Houston and routinely posting double-doubles. It took Terrence a little more time than he probably would have liked, but he's doing his thing now.

I guess Anthony Davis and Michael Kidd-Gilchrist had choices to make—but as the players destined to be the first and second overall picks in the 2012 draft, their decisions were no-brainers. Would I have accepted them back? Yes, obviously. But we would have argued about it.

And the NBA got it right with them. Both are physically gifted, mature, super competitive. As rookies they played like future all-stars.

Of all the players on the championship team, the player who faced the most difficult decision was Marquis Teague, and we struggled a little bit over it. It took him a chunk of our season to figure out the college game. I didn't see a great need, or benefit, for him to then quickly jump up another level. I thought he should stay another year at Kentucky and told him so.

We talked it over, and finally he said, "Coach, I'm going to do this." At that point I said, "Okay, I wish you luck, and I'll do everything I can to help you." I never doubted he was an NBA player, but I feared he was making it harder on himself than it had to be.

When a player decides to put his name in the draft, even if I don't agree with him, my job is to work to get him drafted as high as possible. In the case of Marquis, we made a lot of calls, but no call was more important than the one the Chicago Bulls made during the middle of the draft as it became clear Marquis was going to be available to them at nineteen. They called me to say, "Look, we haven't worked out Marquis, what do you think?" I said, "Do you love Jeff Teague? If you do, you're going to love Marquis Teague. He plays like his brother." I told them all about his attributes but told them to remember that he's only nineteen. The next day, Bulls general manager Gar Forman and head coach Tom Thibodeau said that they took him on my recommendation.

When the Bulls selected him, I was truly relieved. He got guaranteed money. With Derrick Rose hurt all season, and the Bulls' other point guard, Kirk Hinrich, injured some of the year, Marquis had a chance to get playing time, but he wasn't able to seize it. "I wasn't prepared to sit the whole season," he told one of the Chicago writers. "I didn't really expect that. I thought I was going to be able to just go in there and fight for a spot."

Toward the end of the year, Marquis went through fourteen games where he played a total of two minutes. That's what can happen. One of the papers wrote that he had a "redshirt year." I'm not worried about whether he'll have an NBA career. He's got all the talent he needs. But he might have made it a little harder on himself.

When Marquis decided to leave, it just about totally cleared the books on our 2011–12 team. Our entire starting lineup—three freshmen, two sophomores—was headed to the NBA. Plus Darius, our sixth man. The one returning rotation player would be Kyle Wiltjer, who had averaged about twelve minutes a game, though far less than that in the tournament.

CHAPTER 8

HUMBLED

February 16, 2013. No, it's not a day that will live in infamy, but I can tell you that it was a pretty low moment in Big Blue Nation. My team, my fourth at Kentucky—in the season after our national championship—got absolutely obliterated by Tennessee in Knoxville. We lost by thirty points—88–58. At one point we were actually down *thirty-nine points*. We could easily have lost by fifty.

We *deserved* to lose by fifty. I don't even have the words to tell you how bad we were.

We played without our best player, Nerlens Noel, because in the previous game he'd slammed into a basket support at Florida and torn the ACL in his left knee. It had happened on a pure hustle play typical of Nerlens. He had been chasing down a breakaway, trying to block a shot. The injury ended his season. But believe me, it would have made little difference if he had played. Maybe we'd have lost by twenty.

A couple of days later, I was talking to the media back in Lexington, and they were asking me about this debacle and the dismal state of our team. Truly, we looked at this point like we were headed straight over a cliff.

I was at a podium with the usual huge press contingent pointing cameras and microphones at me. I talked about all our various deficiencies. Kids who weren't listening. No bench. No fight. No basketball IQ. And now, no Nerlens. And then I said, "All that aside, we can make whatever we want of this season. Whatever we want to make of it, we can. We can be the story of the year. Of recovery. We can do that if they choose to do that. We don't have to win every game. We just have to see kids getting better and figure out how this team needs to play. And then see how we march on."

Yep, I said we could be the *story of the year.* And just to drive home the point, I amplified that same argument in an item I wrote for my Web site that day: "I went to Mass this morning and had a chance to reflect on where we have come from this season, what we have been through and where we are right now. I believe in this team if our players will compete and battle, which they have the ability to do. . . . Make no mistake about it, we are still in a great position to do whatever we want to do. We can still write our own story."

Here's the funny thing. I absolutely meant that, what I told the press and what I wrote. I believed it. And as irrational as it may seem, when I look back on those words now, a part of me *still* believes them. You don't know if you will win or lose until you do.

I don't give up on kids. I don't give up on teams. I don't give up on seasons. That's bred into me as a coach, a big part of who I am. Only at the very end is there that moment of stark reality: *We're done. We got to the end of our story.*

It had been a while since I'd had a team that struggled so much and was seen to have so grossly underachieved. Six of my previous seven teams, going back to 2005–2006 at Memphis, had won thirty or more games. They'd *averaged* thirty-four wins. The team that didn't win thirty games, my second one at Kentucky, had gone to the Final Four and had won twenty-nine games.

But an occupational hazard of coaching is that if you keep doing it, you'll hit a season that doesn't turn out anything like you expected. When it happens, you can't point fingers or cast blame. You have to look within. You were the guy who put the whole thing together, who tried to right the ship and couldn't.

You have to try to figure out, *What did I do to cause this? What didn't I see? Why couldn't I get through to my team? What do I have to change to make sure it doesn't happen again?*

There were times during the season when I wondered: *Am I the worst coach in the world?* We supposedly had four first-round NBA picks on our team, a lot of talent to have on one college roster, but we rarely looked like we were much better than the guys we were playing. Even when we won.

After two warm-ups at home against Northwood and Transylvania (both were exhibition games), our first real challenge came against Maryland at the new Barclays Center in Brooklyn. Their second-year coach, Mark Turgeon, was doing a nice job of rebuilding, but Maryland was not among the better teams in the ACC and would not go on to play in the NCAA tournament.

We squeaked by them, 72–69, for one reason only: Jarrod Polson came off our bench, played twenty-two minutes, and scored ten points, including a couple of big baskets at the end. Jarrod had started out at Kentucky as a walk-on. The job of those guys is to give everything they've got in practice and make it tough on the guys who play in the games. One of the best things about my job is when I can call up the parents of a walk-on kid and say I was able to put their son on scholarship—and I had already done that for Jarrod.

I was proud of him after the Maryland game, but I can't say it was a good indicator for our team. Jarrod had played just sixty-two minutes *total* in his first two seasons. With the high goals we set, our program is not set up for walk-ons to have to save us.

I'll admit it: This team exasperated the heck out of me. I couldn't get them to do some basic things: Talk and communicate on the court. Get in a proper defensive stance, what we call "staying low." Play under control. Take makeable shots, rather than crazy heaves that have no chance of going in. If you don't have a shot, give the ball up. Run the offense. It's really that simple.

We were ridiculously quiet, and quiet teams don't win. If you walked into some of our practices, you might have thought you were in a library. A couple of times we had guys get tied up in the corner at crucial points of a game, and when they tried to call time-out to keep possession, the referees couldn't hear them. I mean, that's bad, right? You're in trouble, you need a life raft, and you still can't make yourself heard?

I don't need an entire team of alpha beasts (my term for guys like Michael Kidd-Gilchrist and, now, Julius Randle). A mix of personalities is fine. It's probably desirable. If you had eight alpha beasts, you might have actual fistfights at practice. But you need at least one—a couple of them is even better—and this team had exactly none.

They fought me to the end, didn't know how to surrender, and held on to their delusions. One day I got them together and said, "How many of you have played college games and really done anything? How many of you have coached teams to Final Fours and national titles, led championship teams, coached guys who went into the pros, coached in the NBA? None of you? So let me ask you something: Why aren't you listening to what we're saying? Why aren't you talking on the court? Why are you coming out of time-outs and doing what you want to do instead of what *we* want you to do?"

Their idea of what constituted hard work didn't always match mine. How they *felt* was their reality. One day Anthony Davis came back to visit and one of our players said to him, "Man, you wouldn't believe it, Coach Cal has us doing two-and-a-half-hour practices."

Really? I was keeping them out there that long? I don't know what clock that kid was looking at, but we were practicing for ninety minutes. It felt like longer—and probably not just for him—because I had not succeeded in getting them to love the grind. I talked about it, but it wasn't inside them. It's the opposite of "time flies when you're having fun"—if you hate what you're doing, ninety minutes will feel like two and a half hours.

I started to think about the trappings of our program—how we travel, how they are housed. I've always been proud of it, but was it making them too soft? Too entitled? I had to consider that.

"What do you think, that everything is kumbaya?" I asked them one day. "Your life is kumbaya? Don't touch it. Don't question it. Don't push me. This is my life, man. And it's very, very good. But you know what? It's not good. Yeah, you're at Kentucky, you're being treated like kings, but the flip side is everybody's looking at you. You're exposed here, for whatever you are—and right now it's not a pretty picture."

After a while, we just about stopped watching game tape. We were teaching at a level below that. We were telling them, *Here's what you do when you miss a shot. If you're a rebounder, you go back after it. If not, get back on defense.* We had guys who, if they missed a shot, forget about it. It was still in their head. They weren't playing defense on the other end. They weren't blocking out. They weren't getting a rebound.

It got to be all about life skills. When adversity hits you, how are you going to deal with it? We weren't at that point yet of refining how we played and getting to the technical details of stuff you see when you watch tape. I'd say, "How about if we just go out here today and practice our tails off? Let's not think about anything but effort. In the games, forget about all the other stuff. Let's just rebound half of our misses. We do that, and we win? Can we try that?"

Were some of the players coddled before they got here? Yeah. Were they enabled by people back home? Yeah. But that's every year. They're kids, and they come to us having been congratulated all their lives for being good at basketball. In their minds they're months away from the NBA.

I'm trying to push them forward, but at the same time I really did understand that some things for this group were different—different in ways that *were* hard. And, in a way, not entirely fair to them.

Our freshmen had been some of the top-rated players in the high school class of 2012, but what they didn't realize was that the talent level of high school players varies from year to year, and maybe their recruiting class was not the strongest. They were the best of the best—but maybe the best wasn't as good as it had been in some past years. They didn't have the context, the historical perspective, to understand that. And if someone had told them, they wouldn't have believed it.

You hear coaches say all the time, "Expectations for my team are too high. It's unfair to the kids." That can be a cliché. A coach is just buying time, giving kids time and room to develop. He knows full well he's got a killer team.

Here, it wasn't a cliché. Expectations *were* too high.

The so-called experts rated our freshman class—Nerlens Noel, Archie Goodwin, Alex Poythress, and Willie Cauley-Stein—number one in college basketball. I didn't argue with that. Our guys were (and are) full of potential, but there was no comparison between them as freshmen and players like Anthony Davis, Michael Kidd-Gilchrist, John Wall, DeMarcus Cousins, and Brandon Knight as freshmen—or, going back to Memphis, Tyreke Evans and Derrick Rose.

That may seem obvious now, in light of what happened, but I'm not sure a lot of fans understood it until well into the season. Their thinking was more like: *Oh, there's Calipari again with the best freshmen. Guess we'll see him back in the Final Four.* Keep in mind, we lost our top six players from the previous year, all of whom were drafted by the NBA.

There's an old joke that I think comes from guys in the military, which goes something like this: *The food in the mess hall wasn't any good. And there wasn't enough of it.* We had a version of that with this team. My guys weren't playing well and I wasn't happy with them. And I wished I had more of them.

Putting together a roster—assembling enough talent and the right blend of it—is far from an exact science. It's become a lot more difficult in the one-and-done era. By the time I know which kids are leaving and whom I'll have left, I've already assembled the incoming recruiting class—as well as a lot of the guys for the one after that.

I could max out on the scholarships I offer, but I usually don't. The reason is that I don't want twelve five-star recruits on one team—all of them on scholarship and all deserving playing time. It's too many. I'd rather have a rotation of eight or nine. It's workable. Everybody should be happy. But in years that you miss out on some kids you wanted—they make a choice to play elsewhere—you can leave yourself short, and that's part of what happened in 2012–13.

We didn't have enough depth when we lined up to play games. More important, we didn't have enough for guys to really push one another in practice for playing time. As a coach, the bench is your friend. But my hands were tied. I couldn't sit kids down because we didn't have anybody behind them.

The other really unfortunate thing for our young kids was that they had nobody but themselves to lean on. It was kind of a double whammy. Much was expected of them, *and* they didn't have anyone to show them the way. No Darius. No Terrence. No Doron. No Eloy Vargas, a six-foot-eleven senior from the Dominican Republic on that championship team who was a rock-solid, twenty-three-year-old man and is now playing professionally.

We had one senior in our rotation, Julius Mays, a transfer from Wright State who had already earned his degree and was taking graduate courses. Julius was assertive and smart, but his ability to lead was limited because he was in his first year with us. He couldn't really say to his teammates, "This is what's coming next" or "Here's what Coach Cal will expect when we practice over the holidays," because he hadn't been here.

And Julius also had the stigma of coming from a midmajor program. In terms of national reputation and basketball pedigree, his younger teammates far outranked him. (Just to be clear, *I* didn't see it that way, but I'm pretty sure some of them did. Our team would have been a lot better off if they'd let Julius lead them more than they did.)

Early in December we got beat by Baylor at Rupp Arena— pretty soundly, even though Baylor was not nearly as good as they had been the previous season. We suffered what I would say was a "good" loss at Louisville, showing a lot of fight and rallying back before falling, 80–77. Archie was a killer in the second half, scoring nineteen points.

About two weeks later Archie had a nightmare of a game on defense against Texas A&M. Elston Turner, the guy he was "guarding"—and I really do have to put that in quote marks— scored twenty-five points on him in the first half and forty in the game. Turner was a senior; his previous high-point game was twenty-six points. My pride played a part in his performance. We should have trapped him.

We had some good games, some bad. Some games we looked bad even when we won, though I'm always happy for a victory. I'm sure a lot of people assumed it was just a matter of time before we figured it out and picked up steam for another strong postseason. Optimistically, that's what I hoped.

But some of those watching us closely understood that we

had underlying problems we might not be able to solve. Seth Greenberg, an ESPN commentator and former coach, zeroed in on our lack of experience in a column he wrote late in January. "While most fans probably credit super-freshmen Anthony Davis and Michael Kidd-Gilchrist with being the biggest reasons for the Wildcats winning the national title, Kentucky would not have won it without the leadership of three upperclassmen who were invested in winning," he said. "Doron Lamb, Darius Miller and Terrence Jones helped coach the locker room and played with the sense of urgency you need to navigate the season." He diagnosed our various problems—an inability to respond when other teams went on runs, lack of defensive intensity, a penchant for coming out of time-outs and not executing. "The best way to describe this is that Kentucky, as a team, lacks substance, and its players are more self-focused than team-focused," he wrote.

I really wished that I could have disagreed, but he had it right.

A s angry as I was sometimes, my heart went out to individual kids. Archie was one of the guys we were all over. In the beginning of the season he had to play a lot at point guard because the player we were counting on at that spot, Ryan Harrow, left the team for a couple of weeks for personal reasons—which was an extremely destabilizing start for a young team trying to find its footing.

Archie had just turned eighteen. He was six foot four with a lean but strong frame and crazy athletic ability. At times he didn't do a terrible job at the point, even though that's not what he was. But when he got back to his natural position as the "2" guard, he might have felt too liberated. Just about every time he touched the ball, he immediately bounced it, then put his head down and tried to take it all the way to the hoop.

Defenses just collapsed on him. They knew he wasn't pulling up for a jump shot or a floater, and he wasn't passing it. He wanted to dunk everything, but he ended up with lots of double-clutch, off-balance layup attempts and a staggering number of offensive fouls.

If I've got somebody behind Archie, I can say, *Sit next to me for a game. Here's where there's a clear lane and you drive it hard. Here's where you've got Kyle Wiltjer standing by himself for a three-pointer, so please pass him the ball. Here's where you try that six-footer we've been working on in practice.*

Would that be a punishment? Yeah, probably a little, because we can do the same thing by watching film. But mostly it's a learning experience. But I couldn't do it because I didn't have enough depth.

And by the way, it's not like Archie was the only guy who would have benefited from something like this. I had Alex Poythress out there, and in some games, like against Duke early in the season, he looked like the second coming of Dominique Wilkins or some other human highlight film. He was flying around and dunking the ball. Crashing the boards. And there were other times I wanted to grab him and say, "Alex, you've played our sport before, right? This isn't a new thing for you?"

From the first day of the season through the last, I was on Alex about his body language. I've talked about basketball being an intimate game—the five guys on the court and the ones on the bench being like a family. In basketball, just like in a family, you can read the nonverbal cues. (Do you really need your wife or your kid to tell you when something's bothering them? No, you can just see it.) When Alex was tired or unhappy—or when he missed a shot, or after I yelled at him in practice—you could just read it from how he carried himself. He should have been one of our best players, but his demeanor was pulling everyone down.

I said to him, *You've got to change this. You've got to make that commitment.* But I understood that I was dealing with a lifelong habit of his, and in the back of my mind I knew I might only have him with me for a total of seven months. I accept help from anywhere. I don't have all the answers, and in cases where I'm not getting through to a kid, maybe someone else can.

One day Mike Gottfried, a mentor of mine, visited our practice. Afterward, he wrote a note of encouragement to Alex, which I was glad to hand over to him. The subject was Alex's body language—just as Mike, years before when I was at UMass, had made suggestions on how I could improve my own body language. "Alex, work hard to improve your body language," he wrote. "Body language is a facial expression, slouching, dropping your head, how you stand, how you sit, how you speak. Begin today. God created you as a winner and he has big plans for you. Work with him. Be the best. When you feel like you want to drop your head, lift it up. When you feel like slouching your body, stand up straight. When you want to frown or have a sour face, smile. When you feel like complaining, encourage someone else. When someone corrects you, thank God because they care."

I think that helped Alex for parts of the season. I definitely think it helps him as he goes forward.

————

In February Archie came to me and asked if we would write him a letter that laid out how we wanted him to change. That made me happy. It was like when Marquis Teague had come to me, except that Archie wanted it written down, so he could refer back to it.

I sat in the office later with my basketball staff—John Robic, Kenny Payne, Orlando Antigua, and Rod Strickland—and we spent a good forty-five minutes looking at film of Archie's recent games, talking about him, and drafting the letter. We wanted him to make changes that helped us win, and we cared about him. We looked at way too many clips of those spinning, out-of-control shots. "He has to understand that just about every shot he takes is that shot," Kenny said.

Robic commented that even when Archie had a teammate coming his way to set a pick, he didn't wait. He started dribbling the ball, which limited his options. We decided to put in the letter that when he caught the ball, he had to wait a beat—do the old "one thousand one" count—before he did anything. That would give him time to lift his head. If there was a pick coming, it would allow his teammate to get there before he started moving.

We wrote down how he should play when we had a chance to get out on a fast break. First he had to "sprint wide"—run down the sideline so we had proper spacing. When he got the ball, we told him to "recognize numbers." If you have just one guy to beat, we said, take it to the rim. Don't hesitate. If there are two or three back, slow it down. But if you have teammates with you, try to get in the lane, then create a shot for one of them.

This is what we were doing in the middle of the season. On the one hand I was telling kids, "Just play." If you stop them on defense and rebound the ball, or you get a steal, just push the tempo and make something happen. But at the same time I had guys, and not just Archie, whose instincts weren't great. So I had to give them rules. I didn't know if that was a mixed message or not. We were trying to piece things together, but maybe we didn't have all the right pieces.

"Here's what we write at the top of the letter," I said. "You've got to stop being greedy."

I didn't think Archie was a greedy person, not at all. But that's how he was playing, and he needed to see that. I was at my desk, with my staff sitting on chairs around the office. I took notes based on all of our comments, then wrote out the letter. I handed it over to my secretary, Lunetha Pryor, who typed it up, and later that day I gave it to Archie.

I cajoled this team, spoke softly, spoke harshly, reasoned, ranted. Anything I could think of. When I didn't think I was getting through, I tried to get them to make demands of one another. "Would you accept being robbed?" I said. "Well, you're getting robbed. That's what you dudes are doing to each other. What if it was with a gun or a knife? You don't pass each other the ball. What about talking on defense? You don't call out a pick, and your teammate gets his head taken off. Why would you accept that?"

When I tell you we tried everything, I mean *everything*. I stopped wearing ties on game days. I still wore a suit, but with an open collar. The first time I got asked about it was at a press conference after we beat South Carolina at home, which was part of the way through a five-game winning streak for us, the best of the season. We had even won two road games, which is really hard in the SEC—at Ole Miss and Texas A&M. I didn't trust it, but I was happy for the victories.

The reporter who brought up my new no-tie look asked, "Are you afraid you might hang yourself because of this team?"

I laughed, but then I explained my reasoning. My players were sort of tender. I wanted to break down every barrier between us that I could. I didn't want to be the authority figure on the bench, the ogre. That didn't mean I was lowering my standards. Even when we won, I wasn't fully satisfied, which is how you're supposed to coach. You're happy, but you ask for more. You try to get up to the next level. "We shot sixty percent, hold them to twenty-eight, and I'm not totally happy," I said after South Carolina. "I must be a jerk."

One day, instead of having a basketball practice, we played dodgeball. It was the players against the staff. If you haven't had a seven-footer sprinting toward you and firing a ball at your head, you haven't lived. I wore a UK football helmet.

One thing the kids found out, which I already knew, is that there has not been a game invented that John Robic will not come out on top of. Golf. Ping-Pong. Croquet. Bowling. Billiards. He's like one of those old-school gym teachers who just knows how to play everything. He was the last guy standing in dodgeball.

Did dodgeball help us? Maybe a little. We played it the period after Nerlens's injury. We needed a mental break, something to lift our spirits. Everything at that point was seeming like life or death. We upset Missouri after that, on ESPN's *GameDay*, and snuck back into the NCAA tourney picture. We beat Vanderbilt. We showed a little life. In the long run it didn't help, because we had problems that a day of fun couldn't cure.

Right before Christmas we had started using heart monitors to measure effort level. They were small and fit in little vests that went right under the practice jerseys. Members of the training staff, sitting with a laptop at a table in the practice gym, got real-time readouts of heart rates and calories expended.

I got the kids together in our meeting room one day and explained the concept. *The reason we're doing it,* I said, *is to find out how hard we're really pushing. You all think you work hard all the time, and you're not close. This will show what your heart rate normally is, where we want it to be, and what it gets up to when you're on the court. And then there's no argument. How can there be? This isn't to catch you but to show that you can go harder. It's to get you to push through mentally.*

We'll be able to say, "This guy's working. But you're not, so you've really got to step on it." And don't worry about what happens if you go harder. You'll pass out before you die, I promise you.

Some of our players were into it. They'd go over to the guys with the computer and ask, "What was my heart rate?" Other guys would just slink away. They didn't want to know. It was out of their comfort zone, which was to keep on being delusional. They were fooling themselves; they wanted to keep on fooling us.

If you wanted to criticize it, you could say that the monitors helped the guys who needed it least—the ones who were already working. But I was able to go to guys and say, *You're telling me that you're working as hard as you can, but come over here and look at this. Here's your heart rate. Eighty-five percent of maxi-*

mum is NBA rate. That's what those guys have to do in a game. Here are your numbers, and you're never higher than midseventies.

We'd look at the numbers for some of the other guys and I'd point out one who was in the correct range. *You see that dude over there? He's sweating, and his numbers tell you why. You, you're acting like you're dying, but you're not. I'm showing you that right here.*

Competition gets you out of bed in the morning. It makes you alive and it makes you better. It reveals the best and the worst in us. You learn whether you can stand up and respond to being challenged, or whether you back down. When you start getting beaten, you either change or you fail. One of the things I hoped was that the heart monitors would compensate for the fact that we didn't have guys having to compete against one another for playing time. It may have helped some in that regard, but not enough.

The on-court disappointments of the 2012–13 season—our win-loss record, our failure to play what most people would consider John Calipari–type basketball, the way it ended—were self-inflicted. Just to make it absolutely clear, by that I mean they were my fault.

My primary failure was that I did not put together a roster that made my kids compete against one another. They were too comfortable from the moment they got to campus. I had my reasons for letting the roster take the shape it did. In hindsight I can tell you what they were.

One is that I thought Marquis Teague might be with us a second year because he wouldn't be quite ready for the NBA. I certainly hoped he would stay, for his own sake—and maybe I hoped a little too hard. That following season I was hoping the Harrison twins, point guard and shooting guard, would be with us. I didn't want to do anything to mess up their recruitment. And I didn't want whatever point guard I brought in to get caught between the Marquis and Andrew Harrison eras and maybe never really get a chance.

Clever, right? But I paid for it. And if I'm being 100 percent honest with myself, my team paid for it. I am not absolving them of responsibility for how they played, but nothing in my Players First philosophy says that I should protect kids from competition. It's just the opposite. I serve them by giving them competition.

I know better than anybody that just having a group of talented guys is not enough. In college basketball you absolutely must have good guard play—and especially at the point guard position. It's what makes everything else tick.

Ryan Harrow came from North Carolina State and practiced with us that whole championship year, but as a transfer he was not yet eligible to play games. I didn't do him a favor by just handing him the point guard position the following season. Ryan might have been better if he had been pushed for playing time. If he hadn't stood up to the competition and somebody had taken his job, *we* would have been better as a team. Either way, if I'm being true to my coaching philosophy, it's what I'm supposed to do.

If I send my own children out into the world, I have to say, *Look, there are sharks out there. You understand that I can't pro-*

tect you? If you're going to choose to be in certain waters, you have to know how to swim with them. You have to know how to fight and take care of yourself. I can't do that for you.

I've already written about the season when I had John Wall and Eric Bledsoe, both natural point guards. They didn't come crying to me. They relished competition. They worked it out. I'm overjoyed to have Andrew and Aaron Harrison, but what if there had already been competition at their spots waiting for them? I hope they would have decided to come here anyway and fight it out. And if they didn't? Well, that would have told me something.

I lean on Bob Rotella for support and guidance, especially when my team is struggling. Throughout that season he counseled me to just keep trying everything. *You played dodgeball. Just keep trying new things. Be creative and try to reach them in every way you can think of. You can't give up, because that's the one thing you won't be able to live with. Play it out right to the end, and you won't look back with regret.*

Rotella doesn't sugarcoat. One of the main reasons I rely so much on him is that he's a truth teller. I remember him saying, "Look, Cal, you're in this position because of how you recruited. You didn't go for another guard because you wanted those twins. You got what you wanted, but this year isn't going the way you want."

I tell my players to take ownership. Whatever it is, it's yours. I took it off my plate and put it on yours. Rotella was giving me ownership of my own stuff. It's like when I say sometimes that my players like it when I'm "keeping it real"—as long as I'm keeping it real with someone else. When I'm doing it with them, sometimes they don't love it.

That's what Rotella was giving me. The straight-up truth. No one to blame but myself.

I f you look at a tape of the play when Nerlens Noel got injured, it starts out on our offensive end. He's set up near the foul line, we throw him a lazy bounce pass, and one of Florida's guards, a real quick kid named Mike Rosario, steps in front and steals it.

Nerlens is stationary, just about flat-footed as he waits for the pass, and Rosario already has a head of steam. There's not another six-foot-eleven kid in the country who could have caught him—and the vast majority wouldn't have even tried. But we don't have anybody else back, so Nerlens takes off, closes ground, and makes an amazing play to block a breakaway layup. But his left knee smacks into the basket support, and he tears his ACL.

We were already down twelve points at this juncture, and playing lousy. But that's who Nerlens was—our best player and the closest thing to an alpha beast we had. (He played like one but just wasn't vocal.)

He led all of college basketball in blocked shots, with 4.4 per game. He led us in rebounding *and* steals, an almost unheard-of combination, and was among the national leaders in those categories. Nerlens's hands were incredibly quick and, for a young man with a thin frame, incredibly strong—when he grabbed either a rebound or a steal, the ball was his.

We lost that Florida game—the twelve-point deficit became a seventeen-point loss. Nerlens was taken to a local hospital and diagnosed, though our training staff already had a pretty good idea what the injury was even before they carried him back to the locker room.

We waited for him on the plane. When they wheeled him in, he held it all together until he sat in his seat. He was about four rows behind me. I walked back there and looked him in the eye, and he started crying. I got in really close, because I didn't want the other guys to see that he was crying, and I kind of put my head so we were forehead to forehead, and I whispered in his ear.

I said, "Kid, look, you're fine. You have seven million dollars in insurance, so if this is worse than we think and you're never going to play again, you're a millionaire right now, and that's tax free. You can live a great life, kid. The second thing is, I think you're going to be fine, that this is the kind of surgery that we'll have done by the best of the best, and you're still one, two, or three in the draft. The third thing is, if the rehab doesn't go the way it needs to go, you're academically eligible to come back and we'll do it again. Our team is not real good right now, but you're fine."

He laughed when I said that, and it changed what he was thinking. Before that he was panicked. And you can understand why. His mother came from Haiti. They didn't have a lot of money. He had a brother at North Carolina State and one at Boston College. It is a great family. He had a younger sister. But he felt that he was the one with a very big opportunity, and it was right around the corner, but now maybe it had been taken away from him.

I knew that wasn't true. But that's how anyone feels when they're in pain and a little bit of shock. He felt like his life had just changed. He had come down there a healthy kid and now he couldn't move his knee, and he had surgery in front of him.

So I was just assuring him that we had modern medicine. This was a bad injury, but we didn't think there was anything unusual about it. *You can get this fixed and your life is going to be good. Nothing that you've imagined for yourself has changed.*

Teams that have a good mix of talent and leadership and depth—and play really hard—can sometimes rally after an injury takes away their best player. Everybody does a little more. They'll salvage a season. But that wasn't us. To tell you the truth, I think we did well to win any games after Nerlens went down.

Our next game was the fiasco in Knoxville. We came home and squeaked by Vanderbilt, then beat a good Missouri team in overtime. We lost a couple of road games, then scored a big upset in our final regular-season game, at home against Florida.

Obviously, Nerlens getting hurt changed the direction of our team. With him we probably would have been in the NCAA tournament, but we wouldn't have advanced very far. If we'd won one game, I think that would have been about it.

After we beat Florida we might have still been picked for the tournament if we'd won at least one game in the SEC tourney. But we got beaten by Vanderbilt and really didn't give them much of a game. By halftime we were down fourteen, and after that we never even made a run.

If the good Lord had decided that John Calipari needed a season in which he was thoroughly humbled, the final act in our season was the topper. (And please, don't get me wrong, I'm pretty sure God has no hand in postseason scheduling.) We got picked for the National Invitation Tournament. Rupp Arena was being used for the first two rounds of the NCAA tournament, so we got sent off to play Robert Morris—in my hometown of Moon Township, Pennsylvania. A homecoming.

They scored the first ten points of the game. We lost at the end, 59–57, when they hit two foul shots with eight seconds left. I think it's fair to say we were put out of our misery.

But it was good TV. You never get to see the national champs from the previous year get taken out in the first round of the NIT. You don't ever get to see them in the NIT at all. It was a highly rated game—the highest-rated of the whole NIT—and people stayed with it and then even watched my press conference afterward. (My funeral will be large just from the people who come to make sure I'm dead.)

I wasn't upset after the game. I just tried to speak matter-of-factly. I related some of what I had already told the kids, which was "I love every one of you, but you're going to hear the truth in your individual meetings. We will be a tough ball team next year. We will be a tough, hard-nosed, fighting team. I promise you, we will be. Because I can't sit through that again. I can't take it."

Somebody asked me what I was going to tell the players about their status for the next season, with the freshmen we had coming in. I said simply that if they didn't get better, they wouldn't play. They'd play five minutes, not thirty. Maybe some people thought that sounded cold or ruthless. I didn't think so. It was just the truth. I figured they should hear it.

———

Some people said we'd have some kids declare for the NBA draft because they felt pushed by the strong incoming recruiting class. It would be the first time players would make a calculation they'd get more playing time in the pros than they would if they stayed in college. It made for good sports-page stories. It was a way of having something to say about the kids we had coming in, which I didn't mind.

But I really hoped it wouldn't become reality. If you get chased off your college team because you're afraid of the competition, you have no chance of making it in the NBA. None. And in the end, I don't think it's what happened.

Let's start with the guys who stayed. To people who think I just bring in all these NBA-ready kids and roll balls out on the practice court every afternoon for them to play pickup games, Willie Cauley-Stein is an interesting guy to look at. He was more of a football player than a basketball player in high school— a seven-foot-tall wide receiver, if you can wrap your mind around that. He caught fifty-seven passes his senior year and scored fourteen touchdowns.

Willie was considered almost an afterthought in our recruiting class. But we coached him. He worked really hard. He went through a minor knee surgery in the middle of the year. When Nerlens got hurt, he stepped into the starting lineup.

At one point, I'd say, he had a good chance of being a lottery pick. When he got more playing time, some of his limitations became a little more apparent. But he would have been a first-round pick, without a doubt. In his second season he'll have competition for playing time, which I think will only help him. He'll get stronger. He'll develop an offensive game in the post. I don't know exactly where he'll be picked whenever he decides to turn pro, but it will be high. He's a big kid who can really run—he plays hard—and week by week you can see his skills growing.

Alex struggled as much as anybody, and the coaching staff was constantly on him because we knew he had so much to give. He showed it in flashes, then it would go away. There was such a focus on him that I'm not sure a lot of people realized that he put together a solid freshman season. He averaged eleven points a game and did so with great efficiency—shooting 58 percent overall and 42 percent on his three-point shots.

He probably suffered more than anyone from comparisons to the previous season. At six foot seven and 240 pounds, Alex was nearly identical in size to Michael Kidd-Gilchrist. He played the same position, was physically gifted in some of the same ways, came out of high school with a big reputation. He followed Michael by just one year, but he wasn't Michael—and almost no one is.

Alex went back and forth on whether to go the NBA and finally decided against it. I'm glad, even though he probably would have been picked somewhere in the twenties. He'll have guys to really bang with in his second season. It will either kill him or toughen him up—and I'm betting on the latter.

Nerlens chose to enter the draft, which was, with 100 percent certainty, the right choice. If he had come back, he still would have been rehabbing his knee through the beginning of our season. When he finally got into games for us, he would have taken the chance, however slight, of reinjuring that knee. NBA scouts would have seen a still-recovering player, rather than their last vision of Nerlens—an athletic, dynamic force and a defensive stopper.

He got drafted sixth overall, to the Philadelphia 76ers. It's a rebuilding team and he'll get all the time he needs to rehab. Without the injury he'd have been the first pick overall. But he's still better off drawing a big paycheck while he works to get himself fully healthy than he would have been playing part of an NCAA season.

Archie declared for the draft and got picked twenty-ninth, just like Marquis the season before. I had the exact same reaction: relief. I think he took a chance. I just hate the thought of guys leaving us and then going into some kind of limbo, trying to find a pro job somewhere. But Archie squeezed into the first round and the guaranteed deal that goes with it.

He didn't shoot the ball well for us but did in some of his workouts for NBA teams. Phoenix, which picked him, loved his athleticism and his upside. I told him I didn't think he should leave, but he disagreed. Was he right or wrong? He got into the first round, so maybe he was right.

I told Archie he had to work on his game, particularly his shot, and he did before the draft. He played extremely well in the summer for the Suns and may have been the biggest surprise of any of the NBA rookies. It's possible Archie is just one of those guys more suited for pro ball, where the lane is more open and defenses can't pack it in against him, like they did in college.

Two other kids opted to leave, both by transfer—Ryan Harrow and Kyle Wiltjer. Ryan left to be closer to his father, who is having some health issues. He left with my full blessing, and because of an NCAA waiver was permitted to play right away, without sitting out a year, at Georgia State—where he played very well. The change of scenery has worked out for Ryan; he's a good kid and I'm happy for him. Having said that, I don't like it when kids transfer.

But if I'm truly Players First, and a kid believes there's a better coach and a better program for him, I have to accept that. It may, on a personal level, feel like a defeat, but for the young man I sincerely want it to be a victory.

According to the NCAA rules, if a player on your team transfers, you have the right to block him from going to certain schools. Some coaches make a list of places that would-be transfers can't go, usually schools within their conference. Sometimes they include other schools on their upcoming schedules.

I don't agree with that. Who am I to limit a young man's opportunities? He didn't like being with me? That's not automatically his fault. It could be my fault. Does he get to limit *my* options? Come on, give me a break. But these are the kinds of rules we make that aren't fair to athletes.

As far as I'm concerned, if you leave my program, you can go play for Vanderbilt. Florida. Alabama. You can play for Louisville. You have that right. When you come to play against me, I'll give you a big hug. Yeah, I've got that part of me that sometimes wants revenge, and I try my best to keep it under control, but it is never, *never* directed against a kid I coach or have coached. If I ever feel that way, it'll be time to get out of the business.

Kyle was a big contributor to the championship team. The following season he was Sixth Man of the Year in the SEC. At six foot ten he was still better on the perimeter than inside. He had nice post moves and a good touch inside, but not the strength to make room for himself and establish position. On defense he did not move well laterally. Matched up against quicker players, he was sometimes a liability, and there were times I had to get him out of the game because there was nobody he could guard.

He knew all that. He knew he needed to work on his body. He and I talked about it before he came to me about transferring and after he decided to leave. Would he have started for our 2013–14 team? I doubt it. He would have gotten minutes because of his shooting, but would have had to battle for them. One option he had was to stay with us but sit out a redshirt season while improving his athleticism. (As a transfer, he's going to have to sit out a year anyway.)

Kyle grew up in Portland, Oregon, but his father is Canadian, and he has already played internationally for Canada. He made a choice to transfer to a school closer to home—Gonzaga, in Spokane, Washington.

Some people got worked up about it. They said people had made inquiries on Kyle's behalf, trying to find out who would want him if he left us. And I'm supposed to be upset by that? What if that was your kid? Would you want him just jumping off without knowing where he might land? You would want him to transfer without any thought of what was out there? Of course not. If people called some coaches for him, that's what I'd expect.

For me, Kyle leaving was like when one of my guys goes early to the NBA. I give them my guidance, as unbiased as I can make it. And then, whatever their decision is, I give them my blessings.

There are different ways to measure achievement and to keep track of what I call our program's Success Rate. Solely on wins and losses, 2012–13 was not a good year. It was disappointing for me. That's obvious. But if you measure it by whether our players benefited individually, our season was a success.

Nerlens and Archie achieved their dreams and got picked in the first round. If Willie and Alex put their names in, they would have been potential first-round picks. Kyle was Sixth Man of the Year in the SEC.

I couldn't have been happier in August when I learned that Julius Mays signed a contract to play professionally in Italy. You'll remember he was the kid who said that he was his "mother's only son" and wasn't going to fail. He came to us for his last year of eligibility, took graduate courses, and, maybe more than anybody, got the benefit of the Kentucky Effect. Would he have gotten invited to the NBA's predraft combine—where he excelled playing point guard—if he had still been at Wright State? (It made me think I should have played him some at point guard for us.) Would he have gotten a chance to play in Europe? Maybe not. But as a Kentucky player he had more visibility. Having been given an opportunity, he seized it.

In the classroom, we were unbelievable. We had twelve players with 3.0 grade point averages or better. Not just Alex but also Sam Malone, one of our walk-ons, had a 4.0. Our overall 3.4 GPA in the spring was the highest of any of the men's athletic teams at Kentucky.

Twany Beckham, Jarrod Polson, and Jon Hood earned their

degrees. Jon and Jarrod were back with us in 2013–14, while taking graduate courses. Since my first year at Kentucky, we have had a 100 percent Success Rate at graduating players who stayed through their eligibility—ten of ten. If you consider the open invitations we make to players to come back and get their degrees, you can put Wayne Turner and Marquis Estill on the graduates list—making us twelve for twelve in four years. How many other programs can say that?

When underclassmen declare for the NBA, a lot of people think they immediately leave campus and start training and preparing in anticipation of the draft. In lots of cases that's what their agents want them to do. Our guys stay. I ask them to do that for their own good, and also because their academic performance in that last semester figures into our Academic Progress Rate—the NCAA measure of whether our program is moving athletes toward graduation. I say to them, "We made this about you. Now that you've made your decision, I want you to make it about the program and finish the academic term."

To me it is a measure of the mutual respect we develop, even when we have a kid for just one season, that they do what I ask. Nerlens and Archie followed in the tradition of the kids who preceded them and finished their class work. My strong hope for all of them is that over time—during their NBA careers or after—they'll return to school.

'm with my players a lot during the season. It's not all basketball, nor should it be. I'm not a philosopher, a clergyman, a social worker, or a therapist, but I talk to them about their lives, about stuff I think I know. With the basketball thing not working out that well, I might have even done that a little more that season.

One day I got them together and said, *Here's what we're going to do. Every day, you are going to make someone feel good. You're going to call your mom and thank her for something. Or call some-body else back home—your old coach, your math teacher, your high school principal—and express gratitude. On campus, talk to some-one who maybe you don't always pay attention to. Look the person in the eye who prepares your food and say, "Thank you, I really appre-ciate the care that you take."* We went as far as to serve dinner at the lodge to the staff one night to honor them for their hard work.

I know how my life changed when I made it about other peo-ple. It doesn't come naturally for kids to have that attitude. I mean, they're seventeen, eighteen years old. At that age did I think about helping somebody? Not much.

But here, they're in the spotlight, under pressure. Their whole lives are about them, even beyond what's normal for their age group. I think if they can absorb some of what I'm counseling about gratitude, it helps us as a basketball team. That's part of my goal: *Make it about your teammates.*

But beyond that, I hope and I believe they'll remember what I'm saying. If you're a parent, you know how it goes with your own kids—you tell them something, and they might not get it right away. You don't even think they paid attention. But a month later, a year later, you'll see them act in a certain way and think, *Oh yeah, they actually were listening.*

My goal is for every single kid to be better off at the end of the season than he was the beginning. They all get something out of it—on the court, off the court, academically. Hard as the 2012–13 season was, I know that we achieved that.

CHAPTER 9

RECRUITING AT A NONTRADITIONAL PROGRAM

Over the time I'm recruiting a player to Kentucky, I get to know him pretty well. I watch him play. We talk on the phone. There's a home visit. I want to know about him and his family. Who are the important people in his life? Who got him started in basketball? What part of his game does he think he needs to improve? What else besides basketball does he love to do? What does he like to read? What is his why?

I tell him about our university, our campus, and our basketball program. I might tell him a little about my own family. But rather than anything I say, I think what matters is how I make him and his family feel. After I leave a home, that's what's remembered. That guy was real. He was human. He didn't act above us. He cares. Even when they see me on TV, I hope that's what comes across—an impression, a feeling.

It's no secret that recruiting is sales. It's persuasion. But a salesman who's a fake isn't a very good salesman—or at least he's not good at selling to intelligent people. And just like I can't win with selfish players, I can't win with dopes. So I'm not trying to fool anybody. It's about results, referrals, and relationships. If you do right by these kids and get results—and by that, I mean results for them—you're going to get referrals. If you do what you say you're going to do and create trust, you're going to create relationships.

My players have to have the intellect to absorb coaching and the emotional intelligence to be good teammates. When I recruit, I'm already looking down the road and beginning to coach that kid. I'm letting him know how we do things in our program and who we are to one another.

Part of recruiting, not my favorite part, is what is sometimes called "babysitting." You keep calling and checking in with a player, because he has to know you're thinking about him. I'm not great at being on the phone all day. I'm just not. So I don't want to call a kid twenty-seven times. I'll call him once every week or every two weeks. My staff will be in closer touch because it's not my strength. I'm fifty-four, and the kid is seventeen or eighteen. What are we going to talk about on the telephone if I'm calling all the time? It's limited.

But when you get me in the home with the moms and the dads and the grandmas, I'm good. I'm fine. I'm not worried. It's one of the best parts of my job. You're never going to be any good at something if you have disdain for it. My whole thing is it gives me a chance to meet another person and another family. Maybe they come with me, maybe not. But even if they don't, I can give them some information. I can help them in some way.

I was on the phone recently with a mother who was telling me her background, which is amazing. She had her son at eighteen, was a single mom, worked hard, but still struggled at times to keep the lights on and food on the table. She put herself through college and law school. She was telling me about all this, and she started to cry. And I was thinking, *I'm just a basketball coach. What have I done to measure up to her accomplishment or compare to what a lot of the families I meet have had to overcome?*

They don't need me to swoop in and save them. Many have already survived a lot of hard things before I come along. I'm meeting them because they have the great fortune of having a son who is a talented basketball player. They're looking at me and trying to figure out: Is this the man who can help my son take that next step? The family could have its fortunes changed for this generation and for generations into the future. I want to help them get it right. My concern is their side of the ledger. Whom are they going to send him off with? Who's going to be a good steward and make sure this young man maximizes his opportunity?

Some people say, *Oh, that's just your pitch. You're in there knee deep with everybody else, trying to skim off the top of the talent pool, and that's all you care about.* The way I deal with people saying negative things about me: Fine. I agree with everything you say. I'm every bad thing you say about me. Okay, can we move on now? I used to take every opportunity I had to hit back at people, but the older I get, the less I want to be in mud fights. My record sells itself. My kids play well. Their academics are good. They haven't done crazy things on campus.

My whole focus is being straight up with families. I'm not going to lie to them. I'm not going to make promises that I can't keep. I'm not going to tell them that their child, without any doubt whatsoever, is going to be all this and all that—all-SEC, all-American, all-world, first-round pick, top of the lottery. "Everything that he told us when they started recruiting him, it was the exact same thing he told us and proved to us until the very end," is how Jasenka Lyles, the stepmother of Trey Lyles, explained it to a reporter after he committed to play for Kentucky starting in 2014.

Do I let a kid have his own dreams sometimes, however unrealistic, and we'll work it out on the court? Sure. When I recruited Marcus Camby, I asked him, what position do you want to play? The almost seven-foot Marcus looked me in the eye and said, "Shooting guard." I was taken aback, but I wanted to coach him. So I told him: I said, Okay, but you do realize we post up our shooting guards most of the game?

The NBA is the elephant in the room. We don't even really talk about it, but it's there. I tell every player he should plan on staying at least two years. If it's less than that, something good probably happened. And staying three or four years before reaching your dreams is not failing.

As a recruiter, you get a close-in look at families. One thing I've learned is not to make assumptions. To give one example: Is it better for a kid to have two parents? Yeah, I think it is. But I've seen single moms and grandmothers raise a child in a home of great faith and love and be very stern and put up with no nonsense, and that kid turns out the best. And I've seen moms and dads together who enable and coddle. I've seen, at times, fathers living through their sons' basketball careers—not in every case, but it happens.

Maybe they're great fathers in just about every way, but they're in the middle of the kid's basketball life, and it's a problem.

If there's a father or stepfather at home, he's the sports dad. That's just how it works. I've been guilty of it myself. When my kids were involved in soccer or baseball, I'd be telling them what to do and my wife would say, "Stop. Just stop. They're playing soccer. You don't know anything about soccer." And I'd be thinking, *But I'm a man. I know everything about sports, all sports.*

I tell families, *If your child comes to Kentucky, we're not going to talk about how many minutes he plays, how many shots he takes, if the offense I'm running is the best suited for him. In fact, we're not going to talk about basketball at all. We can talk about anything else, just not that. Your job is to love your son. My job is to coach him.*

Later on, when I've got my team all together, I'll ask them: "If we're oh and twenty and you're playing every minute and getting all the shots, are your parents happy or unhappy?" And everybody says, "Happy." "And if we're twenty and oh and you're not playing or getting shots, they're what?" "Unhappy."

Parents are welcome to come to practice and sit there and watch. If they call, I'll talk to them about their kids' work habits, their academics, any of that. I'm usually able to say how proud I am of their son—and how proud they should be. If they get into playing time or any of that other stuff, I make it clear: We're not going there. I'm not doing it, because I can't manage and monitor families and coach a team at the same time, especially with the condensed time we have with a lot of the players.

Apart from their basketball ability—and the academic qualifications required to be admitted to Kentucky and be NCAA eligible—the quality I'm looking for in a kid is *respect*. When his coach talks to him, is he listening and looking him in the eye, or is he staring into space and looking like he can't wait for the guy to shut up? Is he sitting straight up, or is he slouched? Does he notice his teammates, or is he on his own island?

With some kids I've seen, it's like the other guys on their team are invisible. You could show them a mug shot, and they'd be like, *Nah, never saw that dude before.* But he's been on your team for four years. *Really? You've got to be kidding me, man. Let me look at that picture again. Oh, yeah, yeah, I think I do recognize him. What did you say his name was again?*

I don't care how good that kid is. He's not for me. I need to know you're going to help your teammates get better—that you care about them enough to do that. We don't have a star system at Kentucky. If you play for us, you're part of an ensemble. We can't have kids whose main thing is that they want respect. I respected you enough to give you a place in a heck of a basketball program and put you with other kids I think you're going to love. You need to be able to *give* respect.

I look for how kids act in front of the people raising them. If they disrespect their mothers or fathers or grandmothers, that's it. I'm no longer interested. Nothing gets me off a kid quicker. I don't care how good they are. If they don't respect authority at home, there's no way they'll respect their teammates or my authority.

B eing at Kentucky makes it easier to recruit in a lot of different ways. One of them is just the smaller number of kids on my radar. At UMass and Memphis, I always wanted to sign the best of the best, but realistically, only some of them were interested in us. So I was dealing with maybe the top five hundred. I was evaluating them, then reaching out to those I liked and thought I might be able to get.

Now, the question is just, Who are the top fifty players in our eyes? That's all I'm worried about. Let's make sure we touch all of them, and if there are a couple of others who fall outside of that but we think might be good for us, we can go look at them.

What I've achieved in the past was often with undersized guys. Everybody was a little smaller than they were supposed to be, but we won anyway. I'm in a position now where I don't have to do that. If you're not big enough for your position, there's a chance I'll still look at you, but you'd better be a pit bull or an Energizer bunny. You have to play with a speed and a motor that's off the charts. If you're just six feet tall, you've got to be able to put your head on the rim. But there are even exceptions to that. Tyler Ulis, an incoming freshman, and under six feet, is unbelievably skilled—which sets him apart.

A year ago we were looking at a player whom everybody in the country was on, and he said to a friend of mine, "Why isn't Kentucky offering me?" Well, he was an undersized "4," meaning a power forward. So I was waiting to see if he looked like he was developing skills to play away from the basket. If he didn't, he couldn't come with me. I'm not comfortable playing a kid his size at that position, just like I wouldn't put Michael Kidd-Gilchrist at power forward. He might even be good for us there, but there's no future in it. At that size, if he plays around the basket, the NBA never even looks at him because he's undersized for that position.

If he went somewhere else, this kid might really do great. I ran the risk of people saying, *Why didn't you take him?* They'd say

I *missed* on him. That's the phrase. But we didn't miss on anything. We made a decision to let things play out, because I'm not bringing kids into situations where they're not going to succeed.

My strong preference is to wait on players, not jump at them. You've got some coaches offering scholarships to kids in the womb. What are you going to say to the kid who stops growing when he's fifteen? Sorry, but forget about what I promised two years ago? It's why I don't offer scholarships to eighth graders. You don't know what you're seeing. I'm not going to fool kids and tell twelve of them I've got scholarships waiting, and then only follow through with four.

I'm usually not offering a kid until he's a junior. Before that I tell them, *I don't care if you've got offers. If you want to be here, you have to wait. If you don't want to wait, fine. But I want to be sure you are able to play for me. I don't want you coming here and finding out otherwise, so we're going to sit back and see how this thing plays out.*

If I offer a scholarship to a sophomore, it's extremely unusual. He's got unbelievable size and length and a big skill set. He's like six foot ten with guard skills. That carries the day at any level of basketball. He just needs to get stronger, and that happens over time. Or he's a point guard, and the way he is right now, it doesn't matter if he doesn't get any better. He would be good enough. And if he does what he's supposed to, he is going to be outstanding.

There's another category of player that gets special attention: the one who says he absolutely wants to play for me. If you're considered a top kid and you say you want to play for Kentucky, I'm coming to look at you as soon as I can. Why wouldn't I? It means that a kid has been following us. He knows what we do.

He buys into it. If you see recruiting as a form of competition, we've already won. We have this guy already.

Archie was one of these kids. He's from Little Rock, Arkansas, just two hours southwest of Memphis, so he was seeing our games when I coached there. From eighth grade on, he said he wanted to play for Coach Calipari. I mentioned that Michael Kidd-Gilchrist was another. There have been many more.

These guys aren't wannabes. They're not like kids hanging Dallas Cowboys pennants on their walls because they like the uniforms and want to play for America's team. They've thought it out. They have a way they want to play, a style that fits what they do best, and they look at my teams, how we play fast and aggressive, and think, *There it is. That's me. I can reach my dreams with that program and that coach.*

There shouldn't be one legitimate prospect dying to play for Kentucky whom we don't check out. I'm rooting for the kid in this situation. I really want him to be good enough. Ideally, it works out for both of us, but I have to be really careful, because I've felt myself sitting in gyms and rooting too hard. You still have to make your sound judgment.

K enny and Orlando do a lot of the sorting and sifting. They look at the lists that are out there and talk to their contacts around the country. They get the information together, we look at it, and we say, *Okay, who are we evaluating?* We pay attention to the national rankings of players but aren't bound by them. The consensus might be that a certain kid is, for example, the top-rated shooting guard, but once we look at him play, we might have a different opinion.

Eventually, we work our way to our answer to the question, Who should we offer? The entire staff gets involved in that—Kenny, Orlando, John Robic (whom we call "Robes"), and Rod. It's a great group because we don't have different tastes about what kind of player we like. It's not about that. We're together on the type who fits us.

I want to evaluate players in a camp setting or in AAU competition. The AAU system gets criticized, and for some legitimate reasons, but it's better for evaluating players than high school games. Unless it's really steep competition, you get fooled at a high school game. You're watching a kid and he's matched up against an opponent six inches shorter, not as fast, maybe not even a Division III prospect. I can't learn anything from that. If I'm at a high school game, it's usually just to show interest.

I'm on the road recruiting every allowable day. It can be a lot of travel. You sometimes watch five or six games in a single day, then hop back on the plane and move on to another city. I'm not a guy who sits in the bleachers wearing my branded Kentucky gear. It's not NASCAR, where I have to make myself into a human billboard.

It's all become a little crazier—every recruit is like life or death—but still, it's not adversarial when you're in the gyms. All the other coaches are there—Mike Krzyzewski, Roy Williams, Tommy Izzo, Tommy Crean, Billy Donovan—I could go on and on and on—and we talk. There aren't secrets to keep. We're looking at the same guys. Maybe I'll go out with Tony Barbee and Derek Kellogg, guys who played for me at UMass, coached on my staffs, and now have their own teams. You try to make it as fun as you can.

When I go out on the road, my staff has already told me, "Here's who you watch." I used to be looking at ten guys in a game. Now I'm zeroed in on one or two. But even with that being the case, occasionally a different kid catches my eye. He surprises me, and we'll start evaluating him.

We ended up signing two kids at Memphis—Robert Dozier and Chris Douglas-Roberts—after I went to games to watch somebody else and ended up liking them better. Both have gone on to pro careers. It happened recently with a kid we've been trying to sign for Kentucky. This stuff isn't a perfect science. When you go into a gym, you should have your eyes wide open and allow yourself to be surprised.

One of the criticisms of AAU is that players don't get coached, that it's too much of an individual, rather than a team, setting. It's true in some cases. But there are good AAU coaches, just like there are good high school coaches. It's not that big an issue to me.

In fact, some people might be surprised how I evaluate a kid who has been really well coached. I'm happy, because I want to see good coaching on every level. But the individual player might not be that attractive to me if I think coaching has been the biggest part of his success so far. He may be already stretched out. If he's got limitations athletically, maybe he's closer to maxed out than some other kids. Sometimes I'd rather have a guy with crazy, untapped talent because I'm thinking that I can't wait to get ahold of him and see what I can do. *How good can this kid be?*

It's like in any business. If one guy is really educated and has all the right credentials, and the other is hungry and full of passion but still raw, you have a choice to make. I want that second guy. Maybe it's egotistical on my part. I think we can really do something with that kid, even if we only have him for a short time. I want the one with skin in the game. He knows he's got talent inside that's about to burst out, and it just needs to be coached and harnessed.

Another thing I get to observe is how classroom smarts and academic achievement relate to what we often call basketball IQ. I always want a kid who's a good student, but I don't fool myself into thinking that it automatically correlates with being a smart player. It doesn't.

You can be a good student even if you're a slow processor. You read your assignments, study the material, think, and then write the paper or take the test. You might be a person who has to sit there for a while until you have the *aha* moment and you've got it figured out.

A guy like this can be on the dean's list as a student, but he's slow thinking on the basketball court. I've had kids like that, and they can be frustrating, to be honest. You're like, *Why didn't you do that! I know you're a smart guy, and yet we told you this is what you're supposed to do when the other team does a certain thing—and you're not doing it fast enough.* But he actually might not even *see* the situation as fast as one of the other players—or he sees it but takes longer to process it.

You need a quick-twitch intelligence for our game. I'm not talking about quick-twitch muscle fiber—but about how your brain works. You hope a kid like this is also a good student, but to be that, you've got to sit still for long stretches of time. You read, study, contemplate. It's quiet work. Basketball is a different thing.

Our practices are fast-paced. It challenges players to compete off their instincts. Our hope is that a player who is not naturally quick-thinking on the court will become that.

On some staffs, assistants are held directly responsible for signing kids. There are quotas: An assistant must get a certain number of guys, or his job could be in jeopardy. I'm never going to put that kind of pressure on an assistant of mine, where I hold him responsible for the decision of a seventeen-year-old kid.

We don't sign any kid whom I have not personally seen play. There may be someone my staff likes and, for whatever reason, I don't. Over my years of coaching, there have been a couple of times I've taken a player sight unseen, and it was a mistake every time.

Just because a player is good doesn't mean he can play for me at Kentucky. There's a skill set, a toughness, a selflessness, that is absolutely required. There's a demeanor. You've got to be steady, because you're thrown right into it. Packed houses, national TV, intense media attention. Even with the year we had in 2012–13, we led the nation in home attendance for the eighth straight year. We couldn't play poorly enough to drive people away. That might be a hard thing for some kids to deal with, all those eyes on them.

So we choose carefully on that basis, too. I can teach basketball skills quickly, but if a guy isn't mentally strong, I might not be able to change that fast enough.

The gold standard, for me, is the great athlete who has had

great coaching but still has a tremendous upside. He's already really good—he knows how to play, how to use his body, he's got different ways to score—but he's only scratched the surface of his potential.

I felt when I was recruiting them that the Harrison twins fit in that category. Their father coached them well. They trained with John Lucas, the former NBA player who works with pros at his gym in Houston. You have a different challenge with players like that. They may succeed without giving you everything they have. You want to push them as hard as you can, but ultimately their motivation has to come from within.

It's like I said about a Michael Jordan, a Larry Bird, a Magic, a Kobe, or a LeBron (not that I'm putting the twins in that category). They're all-time greats. But they keep grinding to get more championship rings and to get better individually because that's what inside them. They don't know any other way. And they drag their teammates with them.

You have to do some intelligence gathering in recruiting, just as in lots of businesses. Who's helping the kid make up his mind? Is it Mom? Is it Dad? Is there an AAU coach? Is there someone in there whom he's listening to and we're going to have to get to know? You definitely want to make sure a decision hasn't already been made privately, so you don't waste time.

I never know what to say when people want me to describe the recruiting "environment"—or the "scene." It's not a Boy Scout camp. It's not a church choir. It's not a complete cesspool.

It's mixed. A lot of people want the best for kids and have good intentions. Some don't.

Because of where I come from and how I grew up—my family, my friends—I don't see anybody as below me. So I'm going to talk to an AAU coach. I'll talk to other people who are involved. I'll talk to someone's uncle. I may have some doubts about you, but I'm going to talk to you. I'm not going to walk away like you're dirty and I've got to go home and take a shower. I've never been that way. I don't turn my back.

I was in a home where a father had just gotten out of jail. I didn't know what he'd done, but he seemed like a decent guy. All I could assume was that he'd made a mistake. Should I hold it against his kid? Walk out of there and say, *Whoa, this is not cool. Let me hightail it out of here real quick because I don't what to be associated with you, but I hope your son has a good life*?

I'm not putting on a suit and flying to distant cities in order to make judgments on people. But I'm not naive; far from it. There's a difference between walking in a world and swimming in it.

In past years, there were a few AAU programs where I had no success recruiting players. Couldn't even get in the door. The guy running the program didn't like me, or he liked other coaches more. I was closed out. That doesn't happen much now that I'm at Kentucky, because the kids and their families want us in the mix. If we're not recruiting them, they're asking the AAU coach, *Why isn't Calipari coming around?* So if an AAU guy tries to close the door on us, he might be hurting himself.

As a staff, we go into any recruiting situation with our eyes wide open. I ask my assistant coaches directly: *Is there anything going on that's murky?* They'll say, *Well, here are the people around the kid, and here's what we know about them.* I don't have to like all of them. There's always a chance that someone tries to insert himself in some way and the kid and his parents don't have anything to do with it or any knowledge of it.

But you get an overall feeling. If it's too messy, we just walk away. That's it. We're done. I tell every kid, *It's not worth risking everything you've got going on to break a rule.* And it's not worth it for us, either. Nobody I recruit is worth endangering what we've built.

And I've got to be extra careful because it's Kentucky, and because of who I am. I'm the white elephant. I've been under the gun my whole career. I figure I will be again, so the last thing I am going to do is give anybody the ammunition to shoot at me.

I don't entice kids with material things or improper benefits. I'm not going to embarrass myself, my wife, my kids, my university. In my mind it would undermine the coach-player relationship. How can I tell a kid, *I want you to do the right things, even though you and I, we just started off doing the wrong thing together*? From that moment on, I'm not really that young man's coach. I'm a collaborator in something that shouldn't have happened.

I'm going to get into all of this in more detail, but let me say this right here: I'm either the luckiest son of a gun in the world, or I'm not what you think. We get more than our share of great players at Kentucky. Over twenty-some years, I've recruited hundreds of kids to three different schools. I've had players get caught up in some things, but all in all, our kids have behaved well. I don't make promises of any kind that relate to basketball. If you've been promised starting positions, shots, minutes, how does that work? Did I promise other guys on the team the same stuff I promised you? *You're going to be the man. And so are you and you and you.* And then, every afternoon, I'm going walk out on the practice court, whistle in hand, and try to coach those guys?

It's not a team at that point. It's just a collection of individuals, all of them out for themselves. They can't come together because each of them is looking at me, trying to make sure they get what I promised them.

Let me add one thing: There are certain players who are meant to dominate. I've had some of them. Derrick Rose, Tyreke Evans, John Wall, Anthony Davis, Michael Kidd-Gilchrist. They dominated in different ways, but within a team concept. I'm not ever going to shoehorn these kinds of players into an ensemble and say, be less than who you are. I want them to be the biggest presence in practices. I *want them* to take over games when the situation calls for it.

This is not a traditional program. As a matter of fact, we call it a nontraditional program. We are going through things that no other program in the history of college basketball has gone through. No other program is losing five or six players a year to the NBA. We are constantly facing issues and having to make decisions with the thought of what's next and where we are going.

When it comes time to trying to convince kids to come to Kentucky, we have a funny way of going about it. I spend a good bit of time going over all the reasons it might not be for them. It's like the antisales pitch.

The first thing is, you're not going to get thirty shots a game, or twenty. If you want to be the center of attention at all times, don't come here. By taking the fourth- and fifth-most shots during our championship season, Michael Kidd-Gilchrist and Anthony Davis made this a heck of a lot easier to sell. They bought into it totally, and it worked out okay for them.

Also, you're probably not going to play much more than thirty minutes, and that's all you should want to play. That makes us more efficient as a team, and the NBA looks at production per minute. Points, rebounds, assists. How efficient are you? If you play thirty-five, thirty-eight minutes a game, your efficiency declines. You're out there saving energy. If you're a good enough player, you're probably not hurting us, but are you going for every single offensive rebound like you would if I had you on the court a little less?

But some players absolutely *need* to be the guy. After games, they get to talk about their "supporting cast." It works sometimes. If teammates fall in around them—they're good role players—the team can win a lot of games. Or maybe they want to be a trailblazer at a program that's been just middle of the road, and they intend to elevate it. I think that's taking a chance. You get one shot at this. I'd let somebody else blaze the trail and walk right in behind him.

It's common for me to tell kids I'm recruiting that they don't work hard enough and they'd better be prepared for what we do. I tell them straight out: *I'm not seeing enough fight and passion. I'm not seeing effort on every possession. With me you won't get away with that.*

It could seem that I'm begging them not to come. It's not that, but I'm giving them fair warning. Have some kids heard me and figured they'd let the good times roll somewhere else? A place they figure they can put in a year, put up a lot of shots, not get pushed too hard, then run off to the league? Yeah, I think that's happened. And I'm good with it, really good. I want to chase those guys away.

Players get with me, and they find out I meant everything I said. Ideally, I get support from their family or people in their circle. I had a mentor of one of our recent players visit a practice. Afterward, he said to me, "I wanted him here because of what I'm seeing. You're not accepting anything but his best. You're watching. When he tries to get over, you're not letting him. That's why I wanted him here, and that's why he'll make it."

All I could say was, "Do me a favor and share that with the kid. I just want him to keep it in his head why he's here."

Sometimes we hear from a player or his circle that he's a West Coast kid, or he's from New York or Philly, and he wants to play near his fan base. That's old thinking. It's all national now. Just about every game we play, your family and friends can watch on TV. The rare times it's not on, you can probably get it on your computer.

Probably the biggest factor in the success of our recruiting is that we recruit players as a group. I wanted the Harrison twins to play with James Young, so I brought them in for a campus visit together, along with Marcus Lee. They all got excited, and they started to bond before they were even enrolled. They were really recruiting one another.

Most of these kids all know each other already from AAU ball and competing at summer camps. They text all year long. They keep track of who makes visits, who got offers. So this is not something you do with just one guy. You want them to be excited about being together. And it's sort of self-selecting, in terms of the kind of player I get. These guys know they're coming in with a big group of really good players. I don't have to worry that one of them expects to take all the shots. If that's their mind-set, they'd have chosen a different program.

We used to bring one kid at a time to campus, have our upper-classmen act as hosts, and make that kid feel like he was our most important recruit. The current players would give him a thumbs up or a thumbs down. Would he fit in, or not? And it meant something to the current players, because they were all coming back, or certainly most of them were. Now we bring in a whole group, with their families, to see if it works. Will they sell each other? Is someone not comfortable with the group? Do the families get along? It's a whole different concept, based on the new reality that the team turns over much more quickly, and we don't have as many returnees.

You can never be absolutely sure you know everything about a kid you're recruiting—or what he might do once he's with you. Any coach who thinks otherwise is fooling himself. You make the best observations you can. You go to a tournament and watch a kid, and if he's running around going nutty every moment he's not playing, you take note of that. Is that really what you want?

But I've seen guys, some of the most solid kids I've ever re-cruited—good grades, mom's a schoolteacher, dad's some kind of professional—go to college and get caught stealing out of dorms. He's a great kid and he's lifting a stereo out of the room down the hall? Yeah, he did that. You just shake your head.

Lexington isn't a big city. It's on the quiet side. But our players can find trouble if they look for it. They're big and recognizable and have egos. We've been lucky so far. We haven't had anybody do anything really crazy. I talk to them about avoiding the impulse to bask in their celebrity status. I call it "the need to be stroked." My advice is, *Don't go to a club if that's what you're looking for. Go to the mall. They'll love you there. Or get a dog. He'll love you no matter what.*

P eople say they want college athletes to be treated like normal students. Well, they're not that. Not at our level of Division I basketball and not at major-conference college football programs. We could argue the point and say it's not right.

But if you want them to be treated like normal students, let's all do it like Division III and have no scholarships. Do away with all of these schools hopping from conference to conference. Just dial it all down. Get the money out of it. But until we do that, let's deal with reality.

My players live, all together, in a small dorm called the Wildcat Coal Lodge. The name is a reference to one of the major industries in our state. One time I was visiting a coal mine, and I went underground and asked one of the miners, "When do you guys go to lunch? When do you go to the bathroom?" And he said to me, "We all go down together, and we all come up together."

I thought, *Wow, you're talking about a team. You're talking about life and death.* I loved what he said so much that I had the words put on a plaque that hangs near the front door to the Coal Lodge, so our kids see it when they enter.

Their dorm is about thirty steps from the practice facility.

Any time of the day or night that they want to come over and shoot or work out, they can. Guests can visit until certain hours, but no girls are allowed up onto the living floors. If we didn't have dedicated housing, I would not want to be the coach at Kentucky. People on the outside just cannot fully appreciate the level of celebrity Kentucky players have on campus and in the state. The Coal Lodge is new, it's clean, and it's very nice—but it's not Donald Trump nice. It's a dormitory. Another thing we did was totally revamp the locker rooms at Rupp Arena. Our program generates millions of dollars. It gives us the ability to do some things, and I don't apologize for it. Rupp Arena is thirty-five years old and downtown rather than on our campus, and our locker room used to be cramped and not particularly pleasant. We made it into one of the best I've seen anywhere, NBA included. As a matter of fact, the Washington Wizards played an exhibition game at Rupp in the fall of 2013 and one of their players said, "Seeing this, and going back to DC [slumped shoulders], I gotta go back to college."

The floor is the hardwood that we won the championship on in New Orleans. It was donated to us by Northwestern Mutual. We both auctioned additional pieces of the floor for the benefit of pediatric cancer research and for my foundation. There are trophy cases and huge pictures everywhere commemorating high moments in Kentucky basketball. One of my favorites is a photo of John Wall running toward DeMarcus Cousins after we tied Mississippi State in Nashville in our conference championship, which put the game into overtime. It's just full of emotion, and you can see the love between those two guys.

The players' area is beautiful—dark wood, with individual cubicles designed with lots of storage area, because as a neat freak I hate to see their stuff just piled up.

The showers are made to accommodate seven-footers, and each one has privacy, because kids of this era do not like to shower in sight of each other. That's new for me and I don't really get it, but rather than fight about it, I fixed it. They used to go back to campus without taking showers. Now that it's private, I tell them that they must shower before they leave.

Outside, in a common area before you go into the actual dressing room, is the free-throw line where Doron Lamb made the shots that put the game out of reach. Next to that is a lounge with a sitting area and comfortable leather furniture, where our players can come down early before the game and just relax. But one of the intended uses of this area is that our other teams, both men's and women's, can use it to recruit. Before games, after we go in the locker room and then onto the court to warm up, they can have kids in there.

Does this whole complex help us recruit basketball players to the University of Kentucky? Yeah, I think so. A lot of kids might say to themselves, *This program isn't the easiest one to play for. The coach is going to kick my butt. But it's a big-time feel, with facilities that are first class and unmatched. If I'm as good as I think I am, it's where I'll be showcased.*

W hat's changed in recruiting, more than anything, is the speed of the cycle. The normal model used to be that in some years, you were looking to sign four or five guys. The next year you were plugging holes, maybe just signing one or two. It wouldn't be until year three or even four that you were looking for another big group again.

Now, I bring in five or six guys in a year and hope a couple stay. I do the same thing the next year, and then the next and the next. Not everybody's doing it this way. I've sat next to coaches in gyms and they say, "I have one scholarship to give this year, so we're pretty good."

I'm thinking, *That means you've had the same team for three years?* Another guy tells me he's set for big guys; he's just looking for one or two perimeter players. I don't even know what that's like anymore.

No disrespect to any other staff, and their hard work, but the way we do it requires that you give more time and intensity to recruiting. You're on the road more. It's harder, but if you want to compete for national championships, I don't think there's any other way.

CHAPTER 10

I DON'T DO THIS ALONE

(AND I DIDN'T GET HERE BY MYSELF)

T here are different styles of leadership. One is where everyone is a cog, expendable. Slow down and you get replaced. Make a mistake and you're gone, so watch yourself. Your contribution is not singular or special, and don't ever forget that we could get somebody off the street to do your job just as well and more cheaply.

My style isn't that. When we won the national championship, and after any kind of success we experience, I want every single person who works for the basketball program to feel that their personal imprint is on it, that it would not have happened without them. I'm talking about my assistant coaches—everyone who works in the basketball office and athletic department—and beyond, that the dozens of others on and off campus who help us in unseen but important ways.

Am I a demanding boss in lots of different ways? Yeah, I am. My people have to put up with my being a pain in the butt— probably in more ways than I even realize. I have seventeen ideas a day and want them all acted on immediately. I change my mind. I lose my temper. I hope I get forgiveness and that everyone knows that even at my worst, I care.

My staff works ridiculous hours. They're on call day and night. If a player wants to work on a problem with his shooting mechanics at midnight, you'll find Kenny, Orlando, or Robes in the gym with him, rebounding the ball and making fixes. Like I said before, our efficiency in practices—we're not on the court that long—allows time for this. If a kid has a problem or just needs someone to talk to, he knows he can always call one of these guys. Their philosophy is the same as mine—there's no coach and noncoach time. They are mentors, leaders, and friends to our kids every hour of every day.

How I treat my staff is just an extension of Players First. Everyone has to benefit. What we do is not all about the *program;* it's about everyone within it. Nothing we accomplish is worth a thing if people are not appreciated and treated correctly.

The one thing no one on my staff can do is add stuff to my plate. If you're taking stuff off my plate, I'm very happy. But if you're piling more things on, I may have to let you go. I don't want to hear, "Coach, we're having a problem with that bus company that's supposed to take us from the hotel to the arena." Why would you tell me that? If that's part of what you're supposed to be doing, then you have to deal with it.

When it comes to how we make up our staff, I need positive people around me. People with a "we can do this" mentality. I'm not saying everybody has to be whistling and skipping every day, but they have to look at things with an idea that we can tackle anything together. I need people who look at adversity as a challenge and failure as a learning opportunity. I need people with an attitude that we either win or we learn. Even knowing how difficult it is, I can't have negative people around our program.

I also have to be able to trust my staff to do the right things when no one is watching. I have to have people with integrity because if something goes wrong, it's on me and no one else.

Look, what we do—how the outside world measures us—is sports. Basketball games. I never fool myself into thinking that our higher purposes can be achieved if we don't get the basketball part of it right. And the way that starts, the foundation of it all, is that we have to attract talent. Because of that, everyone who works with me must consider themselves recruiters.

When high school kids come to visit us, their eyes are wide open. Just as they get a certain feeling from me, beyond the words I say, it's the same with everyone else they encounter— from the women who sit at the front desk in our suite of offices to the media staff, athletic trainers, and strength coaches. Everyone right down the line.

I don't care what you're doing when a kid and a family come walking by. Stop. Be fully present for them. *How are you? Where are you from? Have you enjoyed your time so far? I love those shoes you're wearing! Make sure to just let me know if there's anything I can help you with while you're here.*

I want a mom to be able to say, *Wow, that was a nice person. That person will care for and look after my son. Whenever I come back here, that's someone I can talk to.*

———

It's important for me that everyone I hire have a certain seat on the bus. In other words, I won't hire the same type of person for five different positions. We need everybody on the bus to do something different—to be put to their best use, what they're better at than anyone else on staff. For example, Lunetha Pryor is my personal assistant and basically runs my life. She knows where I am every moment of the day, no matter what city I'm in. As long as there is something that you add to our team, I'm good with you. I'm always trying to hire people who are strong in areas that I'm weak in, which is why I have a big staff. I'm an idea guy who enjoys being on the court teaching the game, but I'm not the only one allowed to have ideas. A lot of the ideas we present on basketball are introduced to me, but they may have been someone else's ideas, because we are a team in what we do.

I need assistants who will tell me the truth because I can get carried away with stuff I don't need to worry about. For example, sometimes in recruiting I'll be so focused on one or two guys that I'm not seeing the forest for the trees. Someone on my staff will have to tell me, "Hey, we're not getting that kid. I know you're in love with him, but we need to keep an eye on these other kids. They have a lot of talent, too."

If I ever get to a point where I'm being too hard on an individual player, an assistant or someone on staff—or even my wife—will come in and tell me we need to approach what we're doing a different way. If someone can come in and change my way of thinking for the better, I'm all for it. There are times where I'll be too hard on a guy while I'm letting another one off the hook, and one of my assistants will tell me that we really need to lay off the one kid and step on the pedal with the other.

Players sometimes vent to the assistants. They'll come in and say, *Here's what's bothering me* or *Here's how I feel.* It could have something to do with playing time or just something I said to the kid that didn't land right. The player might ask if he should come to me or just let it drop, and the coach will either say, *Yeah, you should* or *Best to let it go.* Or he might suggest the kid sleep on it and they'll see what it looks like the next day.

In that way the assistants are like filters, determining what should get all the way to me. But the staff can't just take the player's side. Their job is to explain what I'm doing and why. It's just like if you're married. You don't let the kids divide and conquer the mom and the dad. You listen, you try to fix what needs fixing, but you don't throw your spouse under the bus.

I told you I don't talk with parents about basketball. To be honest about it, my staff sometimes does. I know it happens. They'll listen, to a point, because maybe a parent needs to feel like they at least got a hearing and let off steam. But I want to be buffered from it as much as possible. I'm happy if my assistant coaches handle it and I never have to hear about it.

Y ou hear people in the profession sometimes talking about open head coaching jobs and which of them are "good." I always say to guys who are trying to move up: *A good job is a job you can get.* Those things are precious. They don't come open that often, and there are usually a large number of qualified candidates.

I'm pretty sure not too many people thought UMass was a good job when I got hired. Where you get that first job isn't usually an easy place to succeed—that's why the position came open in the first place.

John Robic is the guy on my staff I've been with the longest, going back a quarter century to when we were together at the Five-Star Basketball Camp. He was with me at UMass, then stayed on when I went to coach the New Jersey Nets and Bruiser Flint succeeded me. In 1999 he became the head coach at Youngstown. He did a heck of a job in a tough situation, one year winning nineteen games without a great deal of talent. But he couldn't keep it going and got fired.

I hired him back onto my staff at Memphis, then he came with me to Kentucky. You work so closely and over such long hours with your assistants that you become like brothers with all of them, but when you've been together as long as Robes and I have, it's at another level. Professionally, we grew up together. I know exactly who he is. He knows who I am.

Robes knows basketball, the X's and O's, like few others. We all watch film of opposing teams and talk through matchups and strategy. But he is probably in his office, studying that stuff and preparing game plans, more than the other guys because he has the primary responsibility for scouting. He knows exactly what information I need before each game to be prepared to coach—what film I need to watch, what I need to see to understand the tendencies of individual players and the other team as a whole. He knows what I'm thinking and how I'm thinking.

Because John is so focused on game preparation, he's not as active in recruiting as some of our other guys. But he can still recruit, and does.

Kenny Payne had an accomplished playing career—a national championship with Louisville; first-round pick in the NBA; four years in the league; then an overseas playing career with teams on four different continents. I don't know if you've ever seen the way certain former pro athletes carry themselves. Their whole body language, every step they take, sort of says, *Yeah, as a matter of fact, I am all that.*

One of the great things about Kenny is how *unlike* that he is. There's no entitlement. His whole attitude toward the players is: *I'm here for you. Whatever you need, just ask me.* He'll go back to the gym late at night and work them out. He is very good at skill work with our big men, and his tutoring of Anthony Davis was a big reason Anthony became the first overall pick in the draft.

I mentioned that I don't like hiring five guys who are all the same guy with the same set of skills. I don't think there's a staff anywhere that can match the varied life experiences of my three assistants.

Orlando Antigua was born in the Dominican Republic, grew up in New York, and was a McDonald's All American in high school and a collegiate player at Pittsburgh. From there he played seven seasons for the Harlem Globetrotters—as their first Hispanic player ever, and the first non–African American since the early 1940s. One of Orlando's great strengths is that he's loquacious. He can talk to anyone. Not only did he play for the Globies, but he was like their front man—the guy who grabbed the microphone at half-court and did commentary on all the tricks.

Rod Strickland's title is "special assistant to the head coach." He has his eyes on everything we do—practices, games, scouting— and is able to give me counsel based on his seventeen years as an NBA point guard. That's a heck of a resource for me to have around.

Our coaches each have their own expertise. Kenny's maybe a little better with the big guys. I'm on the point guards. Orlando, at six foot seven, played out on the wing and has a lot to say to those guys. But I truly want all my coaches to coach all my players.

The reason for that is I want them to be well-rounded as coaches—to be able to think along with me and see the big picture. Just as I'm trying to develop players, I'm preparing them for the next stage of their careers as head coaches. They just need to be able to afford to take one of those jobs.

I'm not going to get into numbers, but my assistant coaches are the best paid in the nation. The money that comes to me from the camps we run in the summer goes right back out to my coaches—as well as to others who work for Kentucky basketball. When my coaches need time off or a vacation, they just go. (Obviously, not during our season.) We don't have a lot of meetings or other stuff on the calendar. We just work until we can't work anymore.

A lot of revenue flows into this program, because of the fans and donors who support the program, and I'd be a total jerk if it all stayed with me. I want to be sure that there's nobody who's ever worked for me who doesn't say, "Look, the dude takes care of you." I want them to benefit when I benefit. Everything that I get a bonus on I make sure my coaches get a bonus on. So if the university says, "We want to give you a bonus" for this, that, or the other, I say, "Okay. I want it in their contracts."

I try to make their contracts more than one year. I want them to feel comfortable that if I get hit by a bus, they'll be okay.

The two other people who have the closest relationships with me and who touch our players daily are our trainer, Chris Simmons, and our coordinator of men's basketball performance, Ray Oliver. Chris and Ray are like brothers and have been with me a long time. I'd trust them with anything—even my own children.

To do this right, you have to have people around you who support your ideas, share your vision, and help invest in the program. At every stop I've been, I've been fortunate to not only find and create those relationships with people, but build lifelong friendships out of them.

At UMass, the two that stand out are Marty Jacobson and Ron Nathan. Ron went on to become my son's godfather. At Memphis, Fred Smith and Billy Dunavant were always there to support my vision.

Here at UK, that man is Joe Craft. Joe doesn't get involved in any aspect of how we run our program, but he supports me personally in my mission to do right by the players. Joe was the point man and benefactor of our locker room at Rupp Arena and our practice facility—both of which bear his name—and without him we don't have the Wildcat Coal Lodge, either. You can't do this alone, and in most cases, the schools can't get all these types of things done. Joe Craft has made it possible for us to do it, and the only way he made it possible is he shares in our vision to make this a Players First program.

Men are famous for not wanting to ask for help. If we're lost, we'd rather keep driving around in circles than get directions. Some of us don't even go to medical doctors, let alone a psychologist if we need one. I'm not in a position to be that irresponsible.

I do a tremendous amount of reading. I read in the morning, before I go to bed at night, and sometimes if I have a spare moment in my office. I've usually got three books going at a time. I want to stay sharp, to be able to bring new ideas to my kids, and to show them that being curious, and an avid learner, is how a person should go through life. If I have a chance to meet somebody who knows more than me, or knows different stuff, I take advantage every time. I once had lunch with Warren Buffett in Omaha. How fortunate is that to get a chance to spend time with a person like him? (He's a man of simple tastes; we ate at a Kentucky Fried Chicken.)

If you're a coach who truly respects the profession, you have to allow yourself to be coached. It doesn't matter how old you are or what you think you've accomplished. You don't know everything. If you let your success harden into stubbornness, you may actually know *less* as the years go on. You get stupider because you stop listening. Nobody can tell you anything.

I'm a collector of coaches, teachers, and mentors. The ones from my younger days I keep in contact with and never let go. And as I get older, I keep finding new ones.

I feel an obligation to families to do everything in my power to help their sons. Not every kid makes it, but I feel like 90 percent of the players I've coached go on to have successful lives. With the ones who don't, I want to be able to look myself in the mirror and believe that I did everything I could when they were playing for me. I educated myself properly. I brought other resources around the program, people who could talk to them were doing wrong. He was seeing all twenty-two guys. Coach Brown is exactly the same way. He sees every player on the court. He has total recall of it, as if it were videotaped into his brain.

To this day, I know I'm too zeroed in on the ball. I know that about myself. I don't see all the spacing, all the angles, that Coach Brown would see. I'm getting better because I keep working on it, and it also helps that between college and pros, I'm getting close to having coached one thousand games. You're going to get better over time, just with experience.

If you've been around a genius like Coach Brown, you draw on it. You see what's possible, but at the same time you realize that certain guys are unique. They have a different ability to see. You can get better at that if you work on it, but what they have isn't normal, and you're never going to get all the way to their level. You just try to get as close as you can.

You have to be confident about your own strengths, whatever it is that you bring to the table. It's not that different from me telling one of my players: *Here are the parts of the floor where you're good at making shots. We're going to make you better from other spots, but in the meantime you keep running to there, and we'll get you the ball. That's your calling card.*

Larry himself never stops learning. A few years ago, after he stepped down as coach of the Philadelphia 76ers and had a period when he was not coaching, he spent afternoons sitting in the gym at Villanova, watching Jay Wright's practices. No doubt he gave Jay a lot of helpful comments, but anybody who knows Coach Brown understood that he was in there trying to see what *he* could learn. It's a great example to follow.

from a different perspective, who had some knowledge or expertise I didn't have.

I've told you some about Bob Rotella. I met him in the early 1990s through Bob Marcum, my athletic director at UMass and another guy who remains a close confidant. Rotella is best known for working with many of the world's top pro golfers, but he's counseled athletes from all sports. He talked to my kids at UMass about their mental approach to competition, how to handle pressure, how to balance basketball with school—and I've relied on him ever since with every team I've coached.

He stays at my house when he comes to Lexington. He talks to the team and sometimes to individual kids, and I always make sure he's also available to the golf team and other athletes and coaches while he's visiting.

For me it's like I get a mental tune-up when he's around—and when I talk to him in our frequent phone conversations. He'll ask what's going on with my team, and I'll talk about how we're doing and maybe bring up certain players I'm struggling to get to change. If he's on campus, he'll observe that kid the next day in practice or in a game. Lots of times, he'll say something like, "Cal, I don't think you're looking at this right." The kid might be telling me one thing, but Rotella sees something else from his body language or how he's interacting with his teammates.

One of Rotella's books is called *Golf Is Not a Game of Perfect,* which you could apply to basketball or just about anything else. If I'm not feeling good about my team, he tells me not to beat myself up. We talk about efforts I've been making, maybe some other stuff I might try. He reminds me I'm dealing with young kids. It's sports. It's life. I can't always control the outcome.

Any chance I get, I bring different voices into the program. George Raveling, the former college coach and Nike's director of international basketball, is considered a sage by many of us, a wise man of the game. He's helped coach our staff. After the 2012–13 season he spent two days with us at a retreat, where we just talked about everything we do and where we could improve.

I've had Ken Blanchard, another friend and the author of *The One Minute Manager* and other books, talk to teams. He has a PhD in leadership. Tens of millions of people have read his books. I figure a guy like that might say something that will stick with one of my kids, maybe even change his life.

Another friend, coach, and mentor is Del Harris, the former coach of the Houston Rockets, Milwaukee Bucks, and Los Angeles Lakers, and a future Hall of Famer. He's one of the sharpest basketball minds I know. He spent two summers on our campus as my assistant as we trained the Dominican Republic national team, and traveled to South America when we competed for an Olympic berth. My players could see my respect for him and that I sought him out for advice and guidance.

One hope I have is that my players see these efforts and get a lesson in humility. They see that their coach reaches out for help. It doesn't make me weak; it makes me better at everything I do.

f I wrote about every one of my mentors, it would require a whole other book. But I do want to mention a couple of others,

because they're so integral to understanding how I coach and what I stand for. The first is Larry Brown, who is now coaching again in college, at Southern Methodist in Dallas.

The way I ended up on Coach Brown's staff was a matter of luck and timing. In the early 1980s I was a young coach on Ted Owens's staff at Kansas, a volunteer working for no salary. It was a foot in the door. Bill Whitmore, the coach at Vermont, offered me a job as one of his assistants, which I accepted—but before I even got out there, Coach Brown became coach at Kansas and asked me to take a (paid) position on his staff.

Coach Brown had already been head coach of UCLA and of three different pro teams. Bill Whitmore said I had to take the Kansas job. I couldn't pass up a chance to work with Larry Brown. It was a great thing that he did and also a good lesson for me: A person's personal and career aspirations have to be respected. He and I have stayed in touch over the years.

Sports is a tough business. The jobs are hard to get, eas to lose. The established guys have what are sometimes call "coaching trees"—they produce assistants who become h coaches, who then hire other guys from the same tree. If cost a guy an opportunity, it might not come around again. was a chance to become part of Coach Brown's tree an soak up everything I could from a man considered to be a of the game.

One thing I learned from being around Coach Brow there's such a thing as natural talent in coaching. I him to Bill Parcells, whom I got to be on the field wi was coaching the New York Jets. Parcells would blo and tell four guys on offense and three on defen

The other big thing I learned from Coach Brown is that you've got to show your players that you really care about them—about their careers, their families, their happiness. You can be the world's greatest basketball tactician, but if you can't show your love to players, you won't ever get the best from them.

CHAPTER 11

AT WAR? COMMON SENSE VERSUS THE NCAA

I f I am dedicated fully to the kids I coach—to their well-being, to their futures, to their families, I have to say what I feel, what I think, what can't be tolerated any longer, and what needs to change.

First some personal history. Marcus Camby was one of the greatest players I ever coached and a fine man who has grown into a wonderful father, husband, and role model. Our careers, in a way, are forever linked, because he was the first really big-time player I had at a time when my program at UMass was coming to national prominence. He was the kind of person any coach would want on his roster, and that has never changed. This past fall, as he approached his fortieth birthday, he was beginning his eighteenth season in the NBA. At his age, that's a testament to character as much as ability. When I saw him in Washington for a game this year, I looked at him and said, "Your hair is gray. Who is going to retire first, me or you?" His comeback was classic. "When I retire, I'm going to come and work for you." I said, "Done deal."

In 1995–96, Marcus led our UMass team to a number one national ranking and a Final Four appearance, the first in the program's history. He was the Naismith College Player of the Year. We lost in the semifinals to Rick Pitino's Kentucky team, the eventual national champions, after having beaten them earlier in the season.

The following year the NCAA began an investigation into players allegedly receiving improper benefits. Marcus, already in the NBA at that point, was among those named. We advised him, "Talk to them. Whatever it is, it's done now."

We had tried to be proactive because it was the first time I began getting players who were good enough that agents and others wanted to get involved with them. Honestly, it kind of scared me, so the year before, we brought in Dick Schultz, the former executive director of the NCAA, to talk to my team about some of the temptations and dangers. We went so far as to invite Bill Saum, from the NCAA's enforcement office, to come in and interview our players and staff, because we were hearing the same rumors they were. If you are truly Players First, sometimes you have to try to save kids from themselves. But even when you are proactive, it doesn't guarantee that something bad won't happen.

The whole episode was typical of what sometimes happens in the environment of college basketball, but beyond the boundaries of a program itself. Some of Marcus's buddies, along with a couple of agents and "runners"—go-betweens between agents and players—were caught up in it. They were acting in his name, often without his knowledge, and getting cash and other benefits based on what he might soon earn in the NBA. There was not a great deal of money involved, about $1,800 that got to Marcus. Other people probably benefited more than he did.

Do I wish this stuff never happened? Yeah, I do. Do I find whatever Marcus did to be unforgiveable? Of course not. He was a young man from a background in which he didn't have a whole lot of money, and all of the sudden, he had people flying around him who thought he was a future millionaire. Try putting some other kids in this situation—put them on a campus in which everybody is more privileged than they are—and see what happens.

The NCAA "vacated" our UMass Final Four appearance in 1995–96, a word they use that basically means they are changing history. It's as if we were never in the Final Four. That season it was a Final *Three*. The NCAA vacated five games total, all in the NCAA tourney—four wins and one loss. Our record was 35-2 that season, but the NCAA's official record book reads 31-1. Our opponents were not awarded the victories, so it's as if those games too were whitewashed from history.

I have too much respect for the sanctity of athletic competition, the sweat and effort that goes into it, to be okay with that. The games were played fairly, according to the rules. There were other kids on the court that day besides Marcus, and the result mattered to them.

UMass had to forfeit money it got for being in the tournament. Marcus himself reimbursed the school all of it, $150,000. He didn't have to, and no player to my knowledge has done it before or since.

Get this: David Didion, the NCAA's former director of enforcement, told me that without my help the NCAA would never have gotten to the bottom of Marcus's case.

The reason I encouraged Marcus to talk was because I believed the NCAA would be fair with me, my players, and my program. If I had it to do over again, I would not have gotten involved in any way. Marcus talked, and it all started right there. I began to be seen in a certain light.

Am I paranoid to think that the NCAA selectively enforces its rules—that some coaches and programs are cast as virtuous and never get a close look, while others are under a microscope? I think that's the way it has been for a long time.

Sports columnist Dan Wetzel wrote in 2004, "By laying down the law on some, the NCAA looks serious about cracking down on cheats. By ignoring the transgressions of others, it sets up a profitable business model. College athletics is popular, in part, because it has clean programs and dirty ones, black hats and white, heels and heroes. In reality the division isn't so clear, but who cares about reality? This works in wrestling, doesn't it?"

In August 2013, ESPN's *Outside the Lines* took a long look at the three-year tenure of NCAA president Mark Emmert and pointed out the same issue—an enforcement division that regards some coaches and programs with a presumption of innocence and others with a presumption of guilt. According to the report, former NCAA investigators revealed the "targeting of specific head coaches and programs presumed as being 'dirty,' particularly within a separate in-house group investigating basketball."

I'm a black hat. Perfect for the role. I talk a little fast. I took a downtrodden program and quickly elevated it, so that's suspect and needs to be looked at. (If you don't want anyone to think you're breaking rules, the best thing to do is lose a lot of games and get yourself fired. Great guy! Squeaky clean. Too bad he just doesn't have a job anymore.) People said I wore expensive suits, as if that mattered or I were the only guy who tried to look good on the bench.

Do people really believe I burst on the scene, grabbed kids from all the top AAU programs, and convinced them I could make their dreams come true in Amherst, Massachusetts? The better they were, the easier it was for me to convince them that even though they had never heard of the Atlantic 10, our conference, that's where they'd rather play? (Who cares about playing in a Duke–North Carolina matchup when you can be part of UMass-Duquesne?)

But wait a second, you're telling me that's not true? Calipari *didn't* have a fleet of McDonald's All Americans and lottery picks at UMass—and in eight seasons, a grand total of *two* of his guys went on to play in the NBA? He actually had to *coach* those guys?

When you're cast as a black hat, that's your role for life. When the NCAA takes that kind of stance toward any coach, it ends up hurting the school and athletes. That's the collateral damage.

The next team I took to the Final Four was Memphis in 2008—the year we lost to Kansas at the end. It was a terrific team that started Robert Dozier, Chris Douglas-Roberts, Joey Dorsey, Antonio Anderson, and Derrick Rose. The loss to Kansas was only our second of the season, against thirty-eight victories.

There had been questions about Derrick's SATs, which he took in 2007 while he was in high school in Chicago. The administration at Memphis did its own investigation, and found no issues. The NCAA looked into it and cleared him to play. It took a second look and cleared him again. We were, again, proactive, and made sure Derrick did everything he was supposed to do before we decided to play him. Derrick had at least five or six meetings/interviews about this issue. We played Derrick with confidence that it was the right thing to do. Everybody felt comfortable. I found it a privilege to coach a young man with his combination of talent and desire.

A year after Derrick had left us and gone on to the NBA, the NCAA went back into it. The issue was whether Derrick had gotten someone to take the test for him. The NCAA wanted to talk to him again. His response, basically, was, "I'm done. I took the test. I'm not answering any more of your questions." You have to understand that this was in 2010.

The NCAA didn't have proof that he didn't take it. His score was barely good enough to qualify to play, just over the minimum number. Derrick was in the NBA at that point. The players' association advised him that there was nothing in it for him to talk to the NCAA.

Just as in the case with Marcus, there was no evidence or allegation that I had any knowledge or culpability in anything that did or didn't occur with Derrick. The same, of course, can be said for his teammates, the kids who played alongside him in the Final Four. As a head coach, you are held responsible, but it's hard to be held accountable for things you cannot have seen or known about.

If I have to, I'll take bullets for my kids. I'm never going to lay blame on somebody else. Plenty of time—most of the time—it's not the kid's fault when the NCAA starts looking into things. It's somebody in his inner circle or outer circle, somebody speaking for him or trying to profit off him. They might be lying and nothing improper at all occurred.

That's the shame of it all. The kid gets hurt most of the time. His teammates get hurt. In most cases, the archaic rules lead the kids to do the things they do.

There have been instances in which the NCAA has taken actions against kids for what others would regard as acts of charity. Somebody helped the kid's family out for a small sum of money—even a loan that was already paid back. It kept them where they were living. The kid doesn't even know about it. But the NCAA says that wouldn't have happened unless he was a basketball player. In my case, they used a term that's only been used one time in the history of NCAA enforcement to make sure that I was damaged: strict liability. At the time, no one knew what that was. No one had ever heard of it before, nor will they ever hear of it again. But it was a convenient way for them to say, *It doesn't appear you knew anything and you may not have known anything, but you know what, we're going to include you in this because we choose to.* The NCAA said, *By being the head coach, you're responsible for whatever happens whether you knew or didn't know, and we're going to call it strict liability.* The latest from the NCAA enforcement is that it will never be used again.

We all recruit the same kids. They come from the same places, the same AAU programs. They've got the same people around them—a mix of characters whose motivations you do your very best to ascertain. And then you just say a little prayer. You hope the young man coming to you is not bringing baggage.

What scares you is that there are certain things that could have occurred before the kid was with you that you have no ability to know about—and that could have an impact on your team and your kids. You have no control. No one likes being in that situation.

Is his academic record accurate? Did anyone ever give him a free tattoo? If his mom lost her job one winter, did somebody lend her a couple of hundred bucks so she could keep the heat on in the apartment and everybody wouldn't freeze? This is all stuff that can happen before the young man got to your campus.

Sometimes you can take the measure of a person, or an organization, by how willing they are to go to war over stuff that doesn't matter.

On February 26, 2011, we beat Florida at Rupp Arena, 76–68. It was a terrific victory for us, the beginning of a ten-game winning streak and a great postseason. Darius led us with twenty-four points, a career high. We wouldn't lose again until we met Connecticut in the Final Four.

After the Florida win, Mitch Barnhart, our athletic director, came walking toward me. He said, "We have something for you." It was a basketball commemorating my five hundredth career victory—with a big "500" written on it. No one had told me they were going to do that. Right away, I was like, *Uh-oh. This is not good.* I said, "Mitch, you know we're going to hear about this. I can tell you that for sure." He asked me what I meant, and I said, "The NCAA won't like it. They took those games away."

I'm not sure he believed me, but the NCAA did, of course, object. It sent our university president, Lee T. Todd, Jr., a letter asking that the school publicly acknowledge that it was wrong to recognize the Florida win as my five hundredth victory. (Dr.

Todd didn't already have enough on his plate as the leader of a university with about thirty thousand students and a budget of $2.5 billion. He really needed to look into the situation with this basketball.)

The letter was very specific. It said that the university's statement of apology "must be approved by the Committee on Infractions prior to its release." It went on for five pages and used such phrases as "extremely troubling" and "very troubling." It informed Dr. Todd that "recognizing Mr. Calipari for a fictitious 500th win does not properly account for the vacation of wins."

Even though I had at first been taken aback to be given the commemorative ball, I was proud that my university came out strongly in defense of fact and history. Sandy Bell, then our senior associate athletics director and the person in the department in charge of NCAA compliance, wrote in a letter that the ball was meant only to signify what had occurred in athletic competition.

"Our only intention," she wrote, "was to recognize the fact that during his career, Coach John Calipari had indeed led his teams to 500 victories on the court. Regardless of how the 42 victories are statistically noted, they did in fact occur."

I am now very happy to have that basketball. I keep it on a prominent shelf in my office. When you walk in, it hits you right in the face.

What gives me hope is that I believe the tide is turning. The NCAA will soon have to reform itself or it will not remain the dominant force in college athletics. The situation reminds me a little of the Soviet Union in its last years. It was still powerful. It could hurt you. But you could see it crumbling, and it was just a matter of time before it either changed or ceased to exist.

My criticisms of the NCAA are not extreme compared to what's being said elsewhere. I'm just one of many voices. Most of the others have no personal stake. They just don't like injustice, and are calling for major reforms.

I say this with some sadness, because college sports have given me the life I have. The NCAA has been an important institution—from the small-college competition it oversees all the way up to Division I football and basketball. They both serve their purposes.

In the lower divisions students get to continue in the sports they grew up loving, bond with teammates, and benefit from coaching. The big-time programs produce revenue and bind campuses together while also providing educational opportunities. A lot of studies have shown that sports increase alumni giving.

Under the current system many of the top Division I athletes, for the time they are with us, are in something like an apprentice program for careers in professional sports. You can argue about whether that's a good thing or a bad thing, but at the moment, it's a fact. If we're going to pack arenas and stadiums with people watching our players perform—and have universities reap the benefits—the least we can do is meet their needs and treat them all with dignity.

What I think everyone has to keep in mind is that the NCAA and the institution of college sports are not one and the same. College sports are the athletes and their families, the coaches, and the athletic departments. The NCAA runs championship tournaments, interprets rules, and enforces them. Increasingly, its rules are not supported, and its ability to fairly enforce them is in serious doubt.

The criticisms are getting louder, and they're coming from important, accomplished people. Some examples:

Frank Deford, who many think is the best sportswriter of this generation: "Never has the NCAA been held in such scorn, regularly revealed as a hypocritical, bumbling vestige of a time when so-called student athletes were known quaintly as 'letter-men.'" Joe Nocera, an op-ed columnist, in the *New York Times*: "Over the last year, as I've stumbled across one outrage after another, I've wondered when someone in a position to do something about the N.C.A.A.—college presidents, maybe? Members of Congress?—would stand up and say 'enough.' It's getting awfully hard to look the other way."

Taylor Branch, winner of the Pulitzer Prize for his books on the civil rights era and the life of Dr. Martin Luther King Jr.: The "noble principles on which the NCAA justifies its existence— 'amateurism' and 'student-athlete'—are cynical hoaxes, legalistic confections propagated by the universities so they can exploit the skill and fame of young athletes." Some of these comments are harsh. I certainly don't consider the best principles of the NCAA to be cynical hoaxes, but I can see how it might sometimes look that way to someone on the outside. I don't endorse all of what the NCAA critics say. But I don't think the organization—and the institution of college sports—would be under such attack if we made some of the common sense changes that I, and many others, are recommending.

———

ports Illustrated has written over the years about the glory of college sports, and no publication has done a better job of covering the high moments—the bowl games, the BCS championships, the Final Fours. I read it as a kid; I still read it.

When college athletes or coaches have misbehaved, *Sports Illustrated* has been all over that. Lately, the magazine has been turning its attention to the NCAA itself and its enforcement office. If you're looking for signs that the times are changing, that's a big one.

In June 2013, *Sports Illustrated* published a story with the headline THE INSTITUTION HAS LOST CONTROL. It centered on a case involving a Miami booster named Nevin Shapiro, who acknowledged giving all kinds of money and gifts and benefits to Miami athletes. What happened after that is a long, winding tale, but in a nutshell: In investigating this improper behavior, the NCAA enforcement office did a whole lot of improper stuff itself.

If you want to know more about this sordid episode, details are easy to find in *Sports Illustrated* and other sources. Suffice it to say, it's never a good thing when you get criticism from a guy inside a federal penitentiary and it seems like he's the one on the high moral ground.

At Kentucky, we follow the NCAA regulations scrupulously. It's the right thing to do, whether we like all of the rules or not. I don't want my kids or program sanctioned in any way, and I am duty bound not to embarrass the university.

At the Final Four in 2013, I got word that there were some new people in the NCAA's enforcement office who were meeting informally with coaches, just to get to know us and hear our ideas. I was asked by people in my athletic department if I would be willing to meet with them, and I said, "They know I'm crazy, right? I'm going to speak my mind."

We did get together. One thing I suggested is that when the NCAA does an investigation, there should be a separate board of people who hear the evidence but never know the name of the school. It's just "University X" or "University Y." The coach stays nameless. Everybody stays nameless. It's just like how the NCAA already handles the appeals process for drug testing for student-athletes. You want to get rid of selective enforcement? That would take care of it. That redacted report would go to a committee that would decide whether there is an investigation or not. We should do the same for the academic clearinghouse, which rules on initial eligibility. Do it without names of the athletes or the school. Number 117-252 can suit up or not. End of story, no possible allegations of favoritism. I also suggested to the NCAA that if a team has a large number of possible professional players on it, move an investigator to their campus to help the athletic department and coaches police the environment.

My main point is that the NCAA needs to stop being in the business of playing "gotcha." Work cooperatively with universities and athletes. Take a good look at the rules and regulations. Throw out the ones that don't make sense. Stop holding programs responsible for infractions they could not have possibly controlled. Most of all, don't hurt the kids.

The NCAA's fourteen-year television contract for the Final Four is worth $10.8 billon. About $800 million a year. And that is not the only money generated in Division I basketball. There's the ticket revenue from games. Money from the sale of apparel. The dollars that come in from television and radio coverage of regular-season games.

I'm one voice. I don't have every answer, but I know that we have to look for one. Should we give athletes in the revenue-producing sports a stipend? Maybe, though I don't have a plan for exactly how that gets done. We should stop making rules that make it so they can't afford a bus or movie ticket. We don't have to make them rich while they're playing college basketball, but let them live with a measure of comfort at least equal to that of the average kid on campus. That seems to me like common sense and not hard to accomplish.

I think eventually we will see an end to all the conference jumping in college sports, and we'll just have four superconferences representing different regions of the country. It will be mainly the schools in the six conferences known as the BCS football conferences. That will leave us with two options: a fourth division, or total separation from the NCAA structure for universities with big revenue-producing sports. Those are the only two options. My belief is that the fourth division is a short-term cure and that eventually, in time, those fourth-tier teams and their presidents and commissioners will look at it and say, *We can do this job ourselves.* Whether the stipends will extend to athletes at those schools in the nonrevenue sports, and to women's sports, is something that will have to be studied and determined.

I'm sure the traditional basketball-playing schools, even those without football, would still be included in a national basketball tournament. It wouldn't be a competition the public would accept without them.

But the superconferences would come up with the rules that fit us. Take the NCAA rules that make sense, and throw out the rest. Come up with whatever is right for the kids. What's the stipend? What are the academic standards? How do we define amateurism? How do we house them? How do we feed them? It would all have to be decided.

Just start from scratch with a conviction that sports are good to have on college campuses and that the big-time nature of them—the money, the attention, the TV—isn't going away. So how do we do it fairly, so that everyone shares in the benefits? How do we do it so the whole thing gains back the respect it should have?

Think again about the dollar figure of the tournament TV package—*$10.8 billion.* Keep it in mind when I relate this one last thought on the NCAA.

Most players, on many days during the season, are hungry. They don't eat right—and don't eat enough—because the NCAA has very strict rules on how and when we can feed them. This isn't my imagination. The *New York Times* wrote about it in 2012. What follows are a few paragraphs of the story:

> *"The perception, for the general public, is that the day they get to school and get their tennis shoes, they are getting this entry into a world where the horn of plenty is always there for them," said Dave Ellis, a sports dietitian for 30 years, who has fed teams at Nebraska and Wisconsin.*
>
> *This, it seems, is not the case. N.C.A.A. regulations limit colleges to one formal "training meal" a day for their scholarship athletes, whether the athletes are play-*

ing tennis, football or any other sport. A few snacks—
nuts, fruit and bagels—may also be provided, as well as
some nutritional supplements like energy bars.

"Food is placed in the same category as a car in the
N.C.A.A.'s eyes," said Becci Twombley, who coordinates
the meal plans for Southern California's athletes.

Exactly! Whatever you do, don't differentiate. Don't use common sense. You ask extraordinary things of the student-athlete, but whatever you do, don't give him anything a normal student can't have.

I've discovered that my players lose weight during the season, in some cases a lot of it. They feel better and practice better during Christmas vacation—when classes are out, they're here on campus, and we're allowed to feed them three meals a day.

These guys can't always eat when other students do. Their schedules are different. They're not allowed to bring food back to their rooms from the dining hall. At the same time, they are six foot six, six foot eight, maybe 250 pounds—and they're expending thousands of calories a day in our practices and in the weight room. Other athletes at their elite level eat five, six times a day. Did you ever read about how much Michael Phelps or some of those guys eat?

Is the NCAA afraid we're going to make them fat? Give them too much ice cream and chocolate cake? The whole thing really defies sanity. What if I give them water—is that an extra benefit? The level of elite athletics that our players participate in has a direct relation to nutrition. The NCAA's concern is that athletes should eat like normal students.

My own teenage son can go into the refrigerator any time he

wants and grab something to eat—a snack before he goes to bed, sometimes a substantial one. But the NCAA is *very* concerned about how many times a day athletes can get nutrition.

The larger point here, obviously, is not just about food and nutrition. It's about treating athletes the way we would want our own loved ones treated.

Here, just for starters, are thirteen things we can do right now just to improve life for our athletes. Many of these may seem like small things, but they're not small for the kids who play for me. And again, it would have to be determined which schools and which sports these benefits should extend to—but I'm sure that they should apply at the highest levels of men's college basketball and football. Some of the improvements—like just feeding kids correctly—obviously have to apply to everyone. Taken together, I think these recommendations, along with the ideas for reform that others can offer, will eliminate many of the third-party problems we experience. All the agents and hangers-on, hovering around and trying to entice kids, would have less leverage if we put more common sense into the rules that govern how we treat athletes on campus.

One: I talked in some detail about how we feed kids. Let's just keep it simple: The NCAA should drop its oversight of this entirely. Trust us, in consultation with our trainers and medical staff, to keep them nourished and healthy.

Two: Each player should get one round-trip flight home each year. He could use it for the holidays or any other time he wants.

Three: A stipend should be put into effect—three thousand to five thousand dollars a year, whatever a committee of coaches and others decides is the right number.

Four: Immediate families should enjoy the same hotels and flights as their children during the NCAA tournament, and we should pay for it. It shouldn't just be the championship game or the Final Four. No one knows when their son's last game is. (For anyone who considers this extravagant, please refer back to the *billions* of dollars generated by the tournament and consider that TV viewers do not tune in to watch the NCAA president present the trophy.)

Five: If a player is deemed eligible for disability insurance, the NCAA or the school should pay the premiums and a player or his family should be able to take out a loan against future earnings, up to $50,000. He's a high-level athlete and projected first-round pick; the great likelihood is he will be able to pay it back. Forgive the loan if he graduates.

Six: Compliance and enforcement should be moved from the NCAA office to either the conference offices, where they used to be, or to a separate body, which could possibly have subpoena power. The NCAA is great at running championships. That should be its main job.

Seven: Players and families should have access to legal representation by professionals to protect them from unscrupulous people. Under the current rule, you can only have advisers if you can afford to pay them.

Eight: If a coach is fired or leaves a university, a student-athlete should be free to transfer without penalty.

Nine: Let us coaches do the human thing and give our players a small Christmas gift, no more than fifty dollars in value. (Is there any other realm of life in which you are prohibited from giving a gift to someone you work closely with and are as close to as family?)

Ten: Restore the eligibility center, which rules on matters like the Derrick Rose case, to an independent body. Currently, it's a department within the NCAA national office.

Eleven: Our kids represent the university in various ways, and we expect them to act and dress correctly. Allow us to buy them a well-fitted suit, shirt, and tie for special events. Many of my players are of a size that means they cannot buy a suit off the rack. The cost for this, with shoes and a belt, would be about five hundred dollars. An "opportunity fund" set up by the NCAA was a small step in the right direction on matters like these, but the funds available are limited and it is ambiguous how we can use the dollars. This should not count against the fund.

Twelve: Let families purchase championship rings. Right now that would be considered an "extra benefit." Our last championship ring, if our players' parents had been permitted to buy it, would have cost them each three hundred dollars—of their own money! If their son comes here and wins an NCAA title, is there something that wrong with a mother or father wanting a memento of that?

Thirteen: Lastly, as I wrote earlier in this chapter, all investigations of eligibility or possible violations should be handled in an anonymous fashion—that way we minimize selective enforcement.

CHAPTER 12

FAIL FAST

I am either a brave man or a fool to write about a season that, by the time you pick up this book, will have passed. My 2013–14 Kentucky team by now has either met expectations or fallen short of them. It would probably be difficult for us to have *exceeded* expectations, since the freshman class I recruited had some basketball "experts" just about handing us a ticket to the Final Four before we ever played a game.

You already know that's not my measure of success. I hope it has happened, but as I go into this season, it's the same as always. I want us to grow as a team and individuals, be about each other and shared sacrifice.

I already know what some of the determining factors will be. Remember how so many people focused on the freshman class in 2011–12—Anthony, Michael, and Marquis? But by season's end, those paying close attention realized that we could not have prevailed without the quiet, steady leadership of Darius, Terrence, and Doron, our upperclassmen.

Their experience, entering that championship season, was all good. They had played in a Final Four and been part of teams that competed and bonded and were regarded as successes.

The freshmen I have returning this year are coming off a very different kind of first season. Alex and Willie played on a team that—as measured by the high standards and rich history of Kentucky basketball—was not good. It didn't make into the NCAA tourney, then lost in the first round of the NIT.

And their day-to-day experience of playing on that team wasn't great. I wasn't happy with them a lot of the time. They weren't happy with themselves. Sometimes they weren't happy with one another. To be honest, it was hard. It's never fun to be part of something that feels like it's failing.

So how will they respond to that? Will they be able to be the teammates that Darius, Terrence, and Doron were? Can they be the same quiet, steady leaders? I strongly believe they can. Every kid, and every team, is different. They're not going to be exactly like those three guys. But I think they'll fill those leadership roles in their own way.

As preseason practice began, one thing I saw right away was that Jarrod Polson and Jon Hood, both of them seniors, had seized leadership roles—and really accepted the concept of servant leadership. They knew they could not have down days, or practice without energy, because their teammates were looking to them. Two of our newcomers, Julius Randle and James Young, were leading by example. At times, they just took over practices—physically and emotionally, with their intensity and passion, like Michael Kidd-Gilchrist used to do. It was exciting to see.

Every team needs to be coached differently, just as every individual needs something different from me. This team scrimmaged more right out of the box than any of my other teams, probably more in the first two weeks than we normally do in the first five weeks. They needed to be challenged, and to challenge each other. And I needed to see how they responded—and how their individual skills held up—when they were going at each other. We didn't do as much drilling, in some cases because we didn't need to or at least that's what I thought. These guys seemed pretty advanced. I found out, over time, that we did need to review some basics—especially on defense. They needed something in front of them, that challenge, in order not to be bored.

I started saying to them: "Fail fast." Don't be afraid to try things. Don't be afraid to experiment. Fail fast and we'll correct. That's how we can truly find out who we are as individuals, and as a team. Early on, one of our big guys rebounds the ball, bursts out and starts to dribble the ball up court. It hits his foot and goes out of bounds. I said to him, "Good, I'm glad you tried that. It doesn't work. So now you know to outlet it to a guard and run up the court."

If a guy tries something and shows he can't do it, that doesn't mean we're not going to try to teach him that skill. Can he become that player he was trying to be? A big man who can burst out on the dribble? A three-point shooter, in time? Yeah, I hope so. Maybe later this year or next year. But it's not going to be part of what he does for us until he masters it.

What I found out in our early scrimmages was that we were

not a great rebounding team. Really? With two seven-footers, three guys six-foot-nine, a six-eight? But we weren't. A lot of our players were accustomed to just going after the ball and getting it, and didn't know how to block out, which is what you have to do at this level. And we weren't great on defense—as individuals or as a team. Great expectations are fine, but I knew we wouldn't amount to much without better rebounding and defense.

We gained a lot of other information that we could put to use as the season went on. Who could initiate plays? Who could finish plays? Who could attack the basket? We saw some guys who were too erect on offense, so we had to change their posture to get them in a better attacking position. Others wanted to always go baseline. It had worked for them in high school, but in our offense, you have to capture the middle of the floor.

Y ou recruit kids, watch them play, get to know them, but you never truly know what you have until they're on campus and on your practice court. There are always revelations. You hope the surprises are good ones. Some of the things I learned early on about this team: Freshman or not, Julius Randle will clearly be in the role of alpha beast. I think I've probably got more than one of them, but he's a definite. From fifteen feet in, he's vicious. He can shoot the ball from the perimeter, so that will make it hard for a big guy to guard him. If teams put a smaller guy on him, Julius, at six foot nine and a totally cut 250 pounds, can eat him up inside. We'll get him one-on-one opportunities, because I think he's going to be a nightmare of a matchup. At practice, he claps his hands, he raises his voice, he senses the level of intensity. If it's not high enough, he takes it on himself to help elevate it.

One surprise: Julius is a really good passer. I didn't realize that until he got here. If not for the concept of fail fast, maybe we wouldn't have found that out. But our whole philosophy has been: try it. Show us what you think you can do, and we'll step in and refine it. Playmaking was not a big part of Julius's game in the past, but it's something he believed he was capable of, and he was right.

His weakness, if this makes sense, is when he gets away from his strength. Julius has some of the skills of a "2" guard, but I don't want him to be that. He's a blend of a "3" and a "4" and a bear of a rebounder. That still should be his focus.

James Young is a six-foot-seven wing who has a quiet resolve, but he's not a type A like Julius. His strength is his skill set for his size. He can really shoot it, and he can handle it and pass it. You'll see that he'll catch it and very quickly make the right pass, which is rare in a young kid. He's a hard lefty driver, so he has to learn to go in the other direction. He should also be a great defender because of his combination of quickness and size.

I talked about revelations and surprises. James Young is one of them, in that he's way better than I thought. By teaching him to get through bumps and get to the rim—and his understanding that he's stronger than he realized—his game is just exploding.

The thing with James is that we're going to have to get him to a point where he's not afraid to assert himself. Don't sit back. Don't be afraid to make stuff happen. Right now his physical talent and skills are ahead of his assertiveness.

But it's not going to work if we're a team that waits for Julius and the twins to take charge. Those guys might have to back off just a little bit, and the other guys need to step up. That's shared sacrifice. It's how you become a true team.

Of the twins, Andrew Harrison is the point guard and Aaron the shooting guard. I don't know if they came out of the womb that way, if they flipped a coin, or if it's a choice their dad made. It just is. What people will see, though, is that they are old-school guys, similar to John Wall and Eric Bledsoe. Either one of them can slide over into the other role. They are, in the best sense, *guards*. When Andrew injured his knee in the preseason, Aaron slid over and played the point. He could do it, but he found out that his brother's job was a little harder than he realized.

The twins have great size, at six foot six and about 220 pounds. They can both handle it and shoot it. They're both great drivers and know how to use their bodies to get to the rim. I've got plenty to teach them, but they come to me very skilled.

Dakari Johnson is seven feet tall and a load underneath. He's the only kid I've ever coached who wants to be listed in the program as a center. That's a great start already; he knows who he is. He's the one who has improved the most since I first saw him. He's really worked on his body. I found out he's up every morning around 6:00 A.M., working out.

Dakari and Willie will compete for minutes. It's going to make them both better. And there may be times they're out there at the same time. They have very different strengths and weaknesses.

Willie can run the floor but starts the season having no real game in the post. He doesn't set up in there very well with a strong lower body and, once he gets it, does not have one really dependable way to put it in the basket. The one thing we found out is when he squares up to the basket, he's a much better player than with his back to the basket. When he's able to face up, it becomes more about using his quickness and nimbleness—two of his strengths—than being physical.

Dakari is good down low, but we need to get him skipping rope and make him better getting up and down the floor.

Marcus Lee is six foot ten, very long in his limbs, and a shot-blocking and rebounding runner. He's one of those kids who will tell you: *I just want to win. However you want me to contribute, I'm willing.* He knows he's going to be part of something special. When he got on the practice court, I found out he's an absolute pogo stick. Like a young Dennis Rodman. One day in practice I told him to put his head on the rim—and he did, literally. He can guard all five positions. And he's a great kid, who comes every day with a positive attitude and energy.

We need to define his game and see where he's strongest. I think when people look at our freshman class as special, they're thinking about a kid like Marcus. He was in the McDonald's game and the Jordan classic. As physically gifted as he is, he's a number one or number two recruit at a lot of other places. Here, he'll have to battle for minutes.

Derek Willis was my first recruit from the state of Kentucky. He's six foot eight, with a slim build and a very good shooting stroke. He wanted the challenge, which is a great sign. Put Derek, too, in the category of good surprises and way better than I ever imagined. *Way* better. He's so long and lanky and skilled, and competing every day against his teammates has put him on a whole other level. He just plays; he has no fear.

I've talked about fail fast and finding stuff out in our scrimmages, including who can initiate plays, who can finish, and who can do both. Alex is the classic finisher. The twins, Julius, and

James look like they can do both. Jon Hood is a very good finisher. Derek can finish but one thing we found out is that he's not good right now at starting plays—at, for example, putting the ball on the floor from the perimeter and trying to get to the rim. He's tried, so I'm able to say to him, "I'm glad you did, kid, but that's not what you're going to do right now."

Dominique Hawkins is our other Kentucky recruit—and probably my biggest surprise. In leading Madison Central to the state title, he was Kentucky's "Mr. Basketball." He is six feet tall, competitive, and strong like a football player. With his body type and mental makeup, he's exactly what Andrew Harrison will face in games—smaller guys with a low center of gravity, who will try to present a physical challenge. They may not have his skills or pedigree, but they are going to try to bother him.

I thought initially that Dominique might be just a very strong practice player for us. He battled Jarrod Polson for minutes at backup point guard. But early on, because of Dominique's work ethic, which is beyond the norm, and his confidence, I felt comfortable putting him in games. It was tough for him because Jarrod came back as not just a leader—but a vastly improved player. He began in our program as a walk-on, but I don't know that anyone would look at him that way now. He would start for a lot of good Division I programs.

James Young and Alex Poythress will compete for minutes, and just as it did with Willie and Dakari, it should make them both better. It's what we didn't have last year: real competition.

I told our team late in October, before we played a game: "I know some of you think you're starting, just because of who you are. But, no, that's not the case. You're in a dogfight every day. You've got to prove what you are out here."

Playing time will be a puzzle. I've had teams with six starters. This team might have *eight* starters. Some of them have to come off the bench. It's just how it is. You have to convince them that minutes, points, and shots are only about ego. If it's the NBA they're worried about, the pros care about efficiency per minute, so make your playing time count. If you're worried about visibility, we've got half a dozen NBA scouts in our gym every practice, or sometimes more. You're getting evaluated every day.

Nobody is probably going to average more than about thirty minutes a game, and that will be just one or two guys. The sixth and seventh guys will play about twenty-five minutes. The eighth guy might get twelve to fifteen minutes. But it's not a math problem. It all gets solved in our practices.

'll admit that one of the things that sustained me during the really hard 2012–13 season was sometimes fast-forwarding to this team. I would think to myself, *Here comes Julius. Here come the twins. Here comes this whole stacked recruiting class, and they're linking up with some good players who, if they had made different choices, would have been NBA first rounders. Unless we hit some bad luck or I screw it up, we should be good.*

This team was ranked number one in the nation in the preseason polls. I've had six different teams ranked first in the past—three at the end of the season, at three different schools. But I never had a team ranked first going into a season. It's a sign of respect, but also a bit sobering. The other highly ranked teams have much more experience than we do, multiple upperclassmen and starters returning.

I also had to think about how not to repeat mistakes that maybe I'd made in the past. Had I made life a little too cushy? If so, how does that get addressed? One thing I've now done is to create what we call the Wildcat Code. It's a point system. Based on their efforts academically and in their conditioning, the players earn certain privileges. Access to the locker room. Practice gear. And on up from there. My point was, I wanted it all to start anew when they got to Lexington. You may have arrived with your credentials and national reputation, but you're in a dogfight from day one.

I began sending my players regular texts as they arrived on campus in June, just to get them thinking about the components of our program.

> This summer you begin to push your body beyond where it's ever been. You must love the thought of pushing through your comfort level!

> How much do you love the game? How much do you love the process of improving and learning? Be emotionally attached!

> Start your day with an unusual passion. Most people tend to perform at a higher level when they operate from a position of passion!

My mind-set is how can our staff help each of you become the best version of yourself. I must get you to totally enjoy the process and trust where I'm taking you.

Question is will you be a good steward? Will you use your wealth and fame for others or just for you? We will teach you.

Keep doing it together. As the tide rises all boats rise. As we become a great team all will benefit.

Do you want to read about history or make history? We must grow individually AND become one heartbeat.

Your program has a 100 percent success rate! You will be drafted (probably lottery) OR you will get a meaningful degree OR do both.

I was away with Ellen early in the summer of 2013, at the beach in New Jersey, where my family goes to relax. Some of my former players were in Lexington—DeMarcus Cousins, Eric Bledsoe, a few others. They were working out, playing pickup with the new kids, checking them out.

I started getting texts from them. Some were about the twins. *Cal, these two, are you kidding me?* DeMarcus texted me about Julius. He said he was ridiculous, better than he had imagined.

I was excited. I can have an opinion, but I'm not on the court with these kids. The NBA guys who go back and go against these guys, they know. If the kids are soft, if they're not ready, the NBA guys will feel it.

But then I'm thinking, here's the problem. Some of the guys are going to leave. Three of them. Five. Seven. I have no idea. My hope is that before they leave, you watch our season and say, *Boy, do they play hard. They are unselfish. They play for one another and they have fun playing.* If that's the case, this current group will be playing in April.

I'm doing what I know is right: recruiting the best players and showing them what a team is. And that means that every year, I've got to go make a new team. Players First.

ACKNOWLEDGMENTS

I was fortunate to play for coaches who modeled for me what it means to lead young men, and then once I entered the profession as an assistant coach, I learned from some of the best in the business. I landed my first head coaching job because the late Frank McInerney, athletic director at the University of Massachusetts, put his trust in me even though I had not yet turned thirty years old. He and his successor, my good friend Bob Marcum, gave me the tools to succeed. I am equally grateful to R. C. Johnson, the former athletic director at Memphis, and Mitch Barnhart, the AD at Kentucky, for hiring me to lead those two programs.

I have been blessed that at each university where I have coached, a former coach who had experienced great success at that school was available to mentor me. At UMass, it was Jack Lehman; at Memphis, Gene Bartow; and at Kentucky, Joe B. Hall. Without their generosity and guidance, I don't know if I would have had the same level of success. What was achieved at those programs could not have happened without the efforts of the more than twenty loyal and talented assistant coaches who worked alongside me.

I have benefitted from spiritual support, as well, at each of my stops—from Father Jay Maddock in Amherst, Massachusetts; from Ken Bennett, Bishop J. Terry Steib and the staff of the Holy Rosary Church in Memphis; and from Father Mark Dreves and the staff at Christ the King Church in Lexington.

Ken Blanchard, Harvey Mackay, and Bob Rotella have brought me information and wisdom from outside the realm of basketball, and I, in turn, have been able to share some of what they've taught me with my players.

My wife, Ellen, has helped make each of my teams a family, and she and our three children—Erin, Megan, and Brad—have given me the love and support I needed to pursue my dreams.

David Black, my literary agent; Scott Moyers, the publisher at Penguin Press; and Michael Sokolove, the cowriter of *Players First* came together to form a different kind of team—and helped me give readers a full account of my coaching philosophy and how it relates to the new realities of college basketball. Eric Lindsey, who oversees my Web site and social media, played a key support role in the publication of this book.

I also want to thank, by name, every player who has competed for me in my twenty-two seasons of college coaching. They are the reason I do this. They are the ones responsible for everything I have accomplished. I'm grateful, as well, to those who played for me during my time coaching the New Jersey Nets and the national team of the Dominican Republic.

UNIVERSITY OF KENTUCKY BASKETBALL PLAYERS

Twany Beckham	Andrew Harrison
Eric Bledsoe	Ryan Harrow
Willie Cauley-Stein	Dominique Hawkins
DeMarcus Cousins	Jon Hood
Anthony Davis	Dakari Johnson
Darnell Dodson	Terrence Jones
EJ Floreal	Enes Kanter
Archie Goodwin	Michael Kidd-Gilchrist
Josh Harrellson	Brandon Knight
Ramon Harris	Mark Krebs
Aaron Harrison	Doron Lamb

Tod Lanter

Marcus Lee

DeAndre Liggins

Brian Long

Sam Malone

Julius Mays

Darius Miller

Nerlens Noel

Daniel Orton

Patrick Patterson

Jarrod Polson

Stacey Poole

Alex Poythress

Julius Randle

Perry Stevenson

Marquis Teague

Eloy Vargas

John Wall

Derek Willis

Kyle Wiltjer

James Young

UNIVERSITY OF MEMPHIS BASKETBALL PLAYERS

Andre Allen

Antonio Anderson

Maurice Avery

Hashim Bailey

Sean Banks

Arthur Barclay

Earl Barron

Tank Beavers

Antonio Burks

Rodney Carney

Shyrone Chatman

Derek Chew

Kareem Cooper

Modibo Diarra

Joey Dorsey

Chris Douglas-Roberts

Robert Dozier

Rashid Dunbar

Duane Erwin

Tyreke Evans

Shannon Forman

Garrick Green

John Grice

Pierre Henderson-Niles

C. J. Henry

Jeremy Hunt

Shamel Jones

Willie Kemp

Preston Laird

Paris London

Travis Long

Ivan Lopez

Doneal Mack

Chris Massie

Scooter McFadgon

Chance McGrady

Brian Mitchell

Marcus Moody

Simplice Njoya

Anthony Rice

Billy Richmond

Jeff Robinson

Nathaniel Root

Derrick Rose

Roburt Sallie

Jared Sandridge

Matt Simpkins

Shawn Taggart

Almamy Thiero

Courtney Trask

Clyde Wade

Dajuan Wagner

Darius Washington

Shawne Williams

Waki Williams

Tre'von Willis

Kelly Wise

Wesley Witherspoon

UNIVERSITY OF MASSACHUSETTS BASKETBALL PLAYERS

Matt Anderson

Chris Bailey

Tony Barbee

Craig Berry

Donta Bright

Anton Brown

David Brown

Andre Burks

Ross Burns

Ishmael Butler

Michael Byrnes

Marcus Camby

Duane Chase

Charlton Clarke

Ted Cottrell

Dana Dingle

Scott Drapeau

Francois Firmin

Jason Germain

Rafer Giles

Ben Grodski

Cary Herer

William Herndon

Derek Kellogg

Andy Maclay

Jerome Malloy

Jim McCoy

Jeff Meyer

John Milum

Sean Nelen

Inus Norville

Rigoberto Nunez

Tommy Pace

Edgar Padilla

Giddel Padilla

Chris Robinson

Kennard Robinson

Lou Roe

John Tate

Carmelo Travieso

Tory Volpe

Tyrone Weeks

Harper Williams

Mike Williams

Page 1: Clarion University.

Page 2: Top, left: Brad Calipari. Top, right and bottom: University of Massachusetts.

Page 3: Top: University of Memphis/Joe Murphy. Center, bottom: University of Kentucky Athletics.

Page 4: University of Kentucky Athletics.

Page 5: Top: University of Kentucky Athletics. Bottom: University of Kentucky Athletics/Chet White.

Page 6: University of Kentucky Athletics/Chet White.

Page 7: University of Kentucky Athletics/Chet White.

Page 8: University of Kentucky Athletics/Chet White.

Page 9: University of Kentucky Athletics/Chet White.

Page 10: Top: University of Kentucky Athletics/Britney McIntosh. Center: University of Kentucky Athletics/Chet White. Bottom: University of Kentucky Athletics/Britney McIntosh.

Page 11: University of Kentucky Athletics/Chet White.

Page 12: University of Kentucky Athletics/Chet White

Page 13: Top: University of Kentucky Athletics. Bottom: University of Kentucky Athletics/Chet White.

Page 14: Left: University of Kentucky Athletics/Chet White. Right: University of Kentucky Athletics/Barry Westerman.

Page 15: Top: University of Kentucky Athletics/Chet White. Bottom: University of Kentucky Athletics.

Page 16: Top: University of Kentucky Athletics/Chet White. Bottom: University of Kentucky Athletics.

from a different perspective, who had some knowledge or expertise I didn't have.

I've told you some about Bob Rotella. I met him in the early 1990s through Bob Marcum, my athletic director at UMass and another guy who remains a close confidant. Rotella is best known for working with many of the world's top pro golfers, but he's counseled athletes from all sports. He talked to my kids at UMass about their mental approach to competition, how to handle pressure, how to balance basketball with school—and I've relied on him ever since with every team I've coached.

He stays at my house when he comes to Lexington. He talks to the team and sometimes to individual kids, and I always make sure he's also available to the golf team and other athletes and coaches while he's visiting.

For me it's like I get a mental tune-up when he's around—and when I talk to him in our frequent phone conversations. He'll ask what's going on with my team, and I'll talk about how we're doing and maybe bring up certain players I'm struggling to get to change. If he's on campus, he'll observe that kid the next day in practice or in a game. Lots of times, he'll say something like, "Cal, I don't think you're looking at this right." The kid might be telling me one thing, but Rotella sees something else from his body language or how he's interacting with his teammates.

One of Rotella's books is called *Golf Is Not a Game of Perfect,* which you could apply to basketball or just about anything else. If I'm not feeling good about my team, he tells me not to beat myself up. We talk about efforts I've been making, maybe some other stuff I might try. He reminds me I'm dealing with young kids. It's sports. It's life. I can't always control the outcome.

Any chance I get, I bring different voices into the program. George Raveling, the former college coach and Nike's director of international basketball, is considered a sage by many of us, a wise man of the game. He's helped coach our staff. After the 2012–13 season he spent two days with us at a retreat, where we just talked about everything we do and where we could improve.

I've had Ken Blanchard, another friend and the author of *The One Minute Manager* and other books, talk to teams. He has a PhD in leadership. Tens of millions of people have read his books. I figure a guy like that might say something that will stick with one of my kids, maybe even change his life.

Another friend, coach, and mentor is Del Harris, the former coach of the Houston Rockets, Milwaukee Bucks, and Los Angeles Lakers, and a future Hall of Famer. He's one of the sharpest basketball minds I know. He spent two summers on our campus as my assistant as we trained the Dominican Republic national team, and traveled to South America when we competed for an Olympic berth. My players could see my respect for him and that I sought him out for advice and guidance.

One hope I have is that my players see these efforts and get a lesson in humility. They see that their coach reaches out for help. It doesn't make me weak; it makes me better at everything I do.

I f I wrote about every one of my mentors, it would require a whole other book. But I do want to mention a couple of others, because they're so integral to understanding how I coach and what I stand for. The first is Larry Brown, who is now coaching again in college, at Southern Methodist in Dallas.

The way I ended up on Coach Brown's staff was a matter of luck and timing. In the early 1980s I was a young coach on Ted Owens's staff at Kansas, a volunteer working for no salary. It was a foot in the door. Bill Whitmore, the coach at Vermont, offered me a job as one of his assistants, which I accepted—but before I even got out there, Coach Brown became coach at Kansas and asked me to take a (paid) position on his staff.

Coach Brown had already been head coach of UCLA and of three different pro teams. Bill Whitmore said I had to take the Kansas job. I couldn't pass up a chance to work with Larry Brown. It was a great thing that he did and also a good lesson for me: A person's personal and career aspirations have to be respected. He and I have stayed in touch over the years.

Sports is a tough business. The jobs are hard to get, easy to lose. The established guys have what are sometimes called "coaching trees"—they produce assistants who become head coaches, who then hire other guys from the same tree. If you cost a guy an opportunity, it might not come around again. This was a chance to become part of Coach Brown's tree and also soak up everything I could from a man considered to be a genius of the game.

One thing I learned from being around Coach Brown is that there's such a thing as natural talent in coaching. I compare him to Bill Parcells, whom I got to be on the field with when he was coaching the New York Jets. Parcells would blow a whistle and tell four guys on offense and three on defense what they were doing wrong. He was seeing all twenty-two guys. Coach Brown is exactly the same way. He sees every player on the court. He has total recall of it, as if it were videotaped into his brain.

To this day, I know I'm too zeroed in on the ball. I know that about myself. I don't see all the spacing, all the angles, that Coach Brown would see. I'm getting better because I keep working on it, and it also helps that between college and pros, I'm getting close to having coached one thousand games. You're going to get better over time, just with experience.

If you've been around a genius like Coach Brown, you draw on it. You see what's possible, but at the same time you realize that certain guys are unique. They have a different ability to see. You can get better at that if you work on it, but what they have isn't normal, and you're never going to get all the way to their level. You just try to get as close as you can.

You have to be confident about your own strengths, whatever it is that you bring to the table. It's not that different from me telling one of my players: *Here are the parts of the floor where you're good at making shots. We're going to make you better from other spots, but in the meantime you keep running to there, and we'll get you the ball. That's your calling card.*

Larry himself never stops learning. A few years ago, after he stepped down as coach of the Philadelphia 76ers and had a period when he was not coaching, he spent afternoons sitting in the gym at Villanova, watching Jay Wright's practices. No doubt he gave Jay a lot of helpful comments, but anybody who knows Coach Brown understood that he was in there trying to see what *he* could learn. It's a great example to follow.